Trossachs and West Highlands

Exploring the Lost Railways

Other books by the author:

Published by GC Books Ltd
The Lost Railway Lines of Galloway
The Lost Railway Lines of Ayrshire
Lost Railway Lines South of Glasgow
Edinburgh and Lothians: Exploring the Lost Railways

Published by Stenlake Publishing Ltd
Borders Railway Rambles

In preparation:
Ayrshire: Exploring the Lost Railways
Galloway: Exploring the Lost Railways
Fife and Perthshire: Exploring the Lost Railways

Cover photographs:
front : Callander Station looking to Oban 1955 (Hamish Stevenson)
back : Loch Oich tunnel; Glen Ogle Viaduct from below (Alasdair Wham)
Title page image: Luib Station signal box 1956 (Hamish Stevenson)

Trossachs and West Highlands

Exploring the Lost Railways

Alasdair Wham

G C Books Ltd, Wigtown

Dedicated to Joyce Siviter, 1958 to 2006. A tower of strength, an inspiration to her family, friends and all who knew her.

Text copyright © Alasdair Wham 2009

Acknowledgements

My thanks are due to my son Scott for his companionship on the journeys and for production of the maps; to my wife Christine for her continued support and for editing the text; to Hamish Stevenson for contributing the railway photographs taken by him and his late father, for access to his photographic collection and for his many helpful suggestions with the text; to Beverley Chadband (GC Books Ltd) for all her help and support; to Mike Clayton for the layout and design work; to Ralph Rawlinson, David Tough and David Rutherglen for their support.

Additional photographic credits: recent photographs by Alasdair Wham. Other recent photographs David Rutherglen p85 and Claycart Design pp59, 70, 120. Thanks also to the following : late W.A.C. Smith p24; late A. George Ellis pp28, 76, 79; Norman Turnbull p30; Richard M. Casserly pp45, 60 (top), 111 (bottom); late Graham E. Langmuir p47 (top), 94, 100 (bottom), 113; East Dunbartonshire Information and Archives, McEwan Collection, p48; late George H. Robin p78, 83, 97 (bottom), 98 (bottom); late Dr John A.N. Emslie p86 (top). Argyll and Bute Library Service, MacGrory Collection, pp119, 121, 124

Alasdair can be contacted by emailing him at:
alasdairwham@googlemail.com

All rights reserved. No part of this publication may be reproduced, stored in a retrieval system, or transmitted, in any form or by any means, electronic, mechanical, photocopying, recording or otherwise, without the prior permission of the publishers. This book is sold subject to the condition that it shall not, by way of trade or otherwise, be lent, re-sold, hired out or otherwise circulated without the publisher's prior consent in any form of binding or cover other than that in which it is published.

Typeset by Claycart Design: mj.clayton@btinternet.com

ISBN 978 1 872 350 349

Published by:
G C Books Ltd,
Unit 10 Book Warehouse,
Bladnoch Bridge Estate,
Wigtown.
DG8 9AB
www.gcbooks.co.uk
email: gcbooks@btinternet.com

Contents

Acknowledgements — iv

Introduction — 7

Exploring the Railway Heritage — 10

Chapter 1   **Callander and Oban Railway** — 13
    — One Man's Railway
    Dunblane, Doune and Callander Railway;
    Callander and Oban Railway from Callander to Crianlarich

Chapter 2   **Branches of the Callander and Oban Railway** — 39
    Lochearnhead, St Fillans and Comrie Railway
    — The Missing Link
    Killin Railway — Watching the Pennies
    Ballachulish Branch — Anderson's Gamble

Chapter 3   **Loch Lomond and the Trossachs** — 71
    Rails to Aberfoyle — Royal Romances, Decimal Points and Fairies
    Forth and Clyde Junction Railway — Hopes and Dreams

Chapter 4   **Invergarry and Fort Augustus Railway** — 103
    — Burton's Bitter Brew

Chapter 5   **Campbeltown and Machrihanish Light Railway** — 117
    — Coal, Whisky and Tom Morris

Further reading — 126

Useful Contacts and Websites — 127

Index — 128

Maps

The Trossachs	12
West Highlands	38
Campbeltown and Machrihanish	116

Abbreviations

BVR	Blane Valley Railway
CR	Caledonian Railway
C&DR	Caledonian and Dunbartonshire Railway
C&OR	Callander and Oban Railway
DD&CR	Dunblane, Doune and Callander Railway
E&GR	Edinburgh and Glasgow Railway
F&CJR	Forth and Clyde Junction Railway
HR	Highland Railway
I&FAR	Invergarry and Fort Augustus Railway
KR	Killin Railway
KVR	Kelvin Valley Railway
LMS	London, Midland and Scottish (Railway)
LNER	London and North Eastern Railway
LNWR	London and North Western Railway
LSF&CR	Lochearnhead, St Fillans and Comrie Railway
NBR	North British Railway
S&AR	Strathendrick and Aberfoyle Railway
SCR	Scottish Central Railway
WHR	West Highland Railway

Introduction

The 'lost railways' explored in the Trossachs and West Highlands are some of the most remote and dramatic in the United Kingdom. Built through some of Scotland's most beautiful landscape, the routes offered a lifeline to remote communities and the prospect of a brighter future. However the beauty of the countryside was probably lost on the railway builders charged with constructing routes through barren, often inhospitable, terrain. For the engineers the challenge was to decide on a route through narrow glens, across vast stretches of moorland and with gradients at the limit of existing technology. To the railway accountants the challenge was to justify the construction costs often based on dubious and optimistic calculations. Building a railway through sparsely populated land to reach a small fishing port in the hope of developing an increase in fishing business, reflects a viewpoint that accountants usually find only in the bankruptcy courts. This was probably a fair description of the Callander and Oban Railway. However such was the railway mania in the second half of the nineteenth century that many such routes were proposed and often built.

The West Highland Railway, from Glasgow to Fort William, along with the extension to Mallaig and the route from Crianlarich to Oban, still operate, despite the dubious economics. Political influences have conspired to retain the lines for perpetuity. Thank goodness! The journeys on these lines pass through a landscape of stunning beauty, also abounding in myths and legends. Even Harry Potter has had an impact on the attraction of these routes and helps to fill trains with loads of the young at heart, of all ages, as they wait to cross the Glenfinnan Viaduct. This then is a special land and the story of the lost railways is one worth exploring.

The Trossachs and West Highlands is a vast area. The West Highlands stretch from Kintyre in the south-west, north to the Great Glen—the geological fault line which links Fort William to Inverness. Many famous islands, such as Islay, Mull and Skye, to name but a few, lie off the rugged and indented western coast. Further south, the area known as the Trossachs is centred on Loch Lomond. Now part of the Loch Lomond and Trossachs National Park, the Trossachs straddles the Highland Boundary Fault line where Highland hills meet with the lowlands.

The expansion of the railways into the area began once there was a railway operating between Stirling and Perth, which served as an arterial route with branches being promoted towards towns wishing to link up with the new mode of transport. When the railway age arrived, Stirling was always going to be an important town with its central location and a route from Stirling to the west coast was soon promoted. The Forth and Clyde Junction Railway built mainly through the flat land of the Carse of Stirling linked Stirling to the Vale of Leven, near Loch Lomond, and opened in 1856. The promoters envisaged a line carrying coal, slate and agricultural produce along with a hoped-for tourist bonanza. The possibility of carrying imports landed at the Clyde ports was also thought possible. Both the North British Railway and the Caledonian Railway competed to secure the route with the former being eventually successful. However, with other rail developments along the Clyde the railway never prospered and closed completely in 1959.

Another route, this time winding north from Glasgow, passing through Kirkintilloch, around the Campsie Fells and across the Carse of Stirling to reach Aberfoyle evolved with several small companies linking up. The Campsie Glen Railway (1858), the Blane Valley Railway (1866) and the Aberfoyle and Strathendrick Railway (1882) even merged for a short stretch with the Forth and Clyde Junction Railway to reach Aberfoyle at the edge of the Highlands. Soon the North British Railway took them under its control, but again the route failed to prosper, defeated by the circuitous route forced on it by the geography of the land and the rise of the motor car.

Quite early on, the Trossachs became accessible by rail from both Glasgow and Edinburgh. Even in the nineteenth century this was prime tourist country, to those exploring the tartan and clan history largely created by Sir Walter Scott and home to the legendary Rob Roy Macgregor. It was a land of drove roads, cattle rustling and illicit whisky stills – it's easy to get caught up in the romance of the area but your abiding memory will be of the natural beauty. This is Scotland at its most enchanting and within reach of the populous central belt.

The Carse of Stirling posed few problems for railway builders, but to the north there was a sharp contrast with narrow valleys, difficult gradients and many lochs to work around. It was also a land with few people but the prospect of an alternative route to the Highland capital of Inverness from the west and then through the Great Glen proved a great attraction. The Highland Railway fiercely protected the route between Perth and Inverness for itself, and the prospect of an alternative route to challenge the Highland Railway's monopoly was a common theme for railway planners. From the Glasgow and North Western Railway's doomed attempt in the 1880s to the building of the Invergarry and Fort Augustus Railway at the turn of the twentieth century many sought to reach Inverness. The construction of the latter, opened in 1903, was a massive gamble and an expensive failure.

Edging eastwards from Dunblane, the Dunblane, Doune and Callander Railway opened in 1858. The route across undulating plains linked Callander with the rest of the railway network. Callander, another part of the Trossachs romanticised by Sir Walter Scott, was beginning to attract the attention of tourists. North of Callander all changed. Here the land rose from plain to foothills and then to mountain passes. The fact that a railway was built north to Crianlarich and then west to Oban was due to one man, John Anderson, whose single minded devotion to a vision ensured that the Callander and Oban Railway was built despite luke warm backing from the Caledonian Railway who had inherited the plan and saw little merit in it. In time, the West Highland Railway was opened and the two lines crossed but famously did not cooperate at Crianlarich, neither wishing to give up running powers on their own routes. During 1965 a rock fall in Glen Ogle hurried the closure of the Callander and Oban route between Dunblane and Crianlarich by a few weeks.

Anderson was involved in the development of a short branch to Killin at the western edge of Loch Tay in 1886 and the construction of the railway to Ballachulish in 1903. In 1905 a further railway formed a junction with the Callander and Oban Railway near Balquhidder in the remote glen south of Lochearnhead: the Comrie, St Fillans and Lochearnhead Railway being the final section of the railway built from Perth through Crieff. The railway network created allowed visitors to arrive from all over Scotland and further afield. Many tours to different destinations were planned and heavily promoted but their popularity was limited, as road transport provided a more flexible rival. The branches were closed by 1966.

To ensure that the complete story of the railway routes included in the book are described I have extended the traditional boundary lines of the Trossachs and West Highlands and have started as far south as Kirkintilloch and as far east as Stirling. Isolated railways like the narrow gauge Campbeltown and Machrihanish Light Railway have been included. This remote railway, the nearest railway to it is in Northern Ireland, was located near the southern tip of Kintyre and began operations in 1877 but it was in 1906 that it first carried passengers. Two other narrow gauge systems, both operated by the British Aluminium Company at Kinlochleven and Fort William have not been explored. I considered the access, particularly to the Fort William to Loch Treig route, too difficult to include. The short section of the Kinlochleven route from the pier to the site of the former aluminium works is a recognised walk but the rest of the railway system in the hills behind Kinlochleven is not explored.

With careful planning, and maybe even the use of the surviving lines, the exploration of the disused routes will help you to appreciate the stunning scenery and marvel at the challenges overcome in their construction. You will also be amazed at how the promoters ever expected to make a profit.

Exploring the Railway Heritage

A surprising amount of railway heritage remains in the Trossachs and West Highlands and hopefully this book will help you to both recognise and appreciate it.

The following points are intended to encourage responsible exploration.

1. Please do not assume that because a journey or place is described in this book that you have permission to follow in my footsteps. This book is not intended as a book of walks. Unless a route has been recognised as an official walkway then the fact that I have been able to follow most of the routes is not meant to imply that a right of way exists or that they are suitable for walking. Fortunately, many of the walks in the area are recognised cyclepaths.

2. If you do intend to trace any part of a route, where possible seek permission from the landowner who will probably be pleased to let you walk the trackbed. Being a responsible explorer will promote goodwill and allow others to follow in your footsteps. Seek permission where possible and respect the Country Code. Access will always depend on courtesy and mutual trust.

3. Many former station buildings are now private residences and while owners are usually pleased to talk about the history of their properties, there is no right of access. No-one wants a walker in their back garden.

4. Always keep away from dangerous structures. Most of the viaducts, bridges and tunnels have not been maintained for over thirty years, some a lot longer. Do not cross fences or barriers erected for your safety.

5. If possible, check out a route beforehand especially in country areas and be prepared for unexpected detours. All distances given are approximate. A missing bridge can result in a lengthy detour. Use an up-to-date map. I have found the Ordnance Survey Explorer series to be the most useful.

6. Be aware of the weather. In Scotland it can change very quickly. Be equipped and in the more remote sections, check the bus times carefully or arrange for someone to pick you up.

The scenery is superb and there is plenty for historians, industrial archaeologists, those with memories of the railway era or simply for the curious to enjoy.

Map of Trossachs

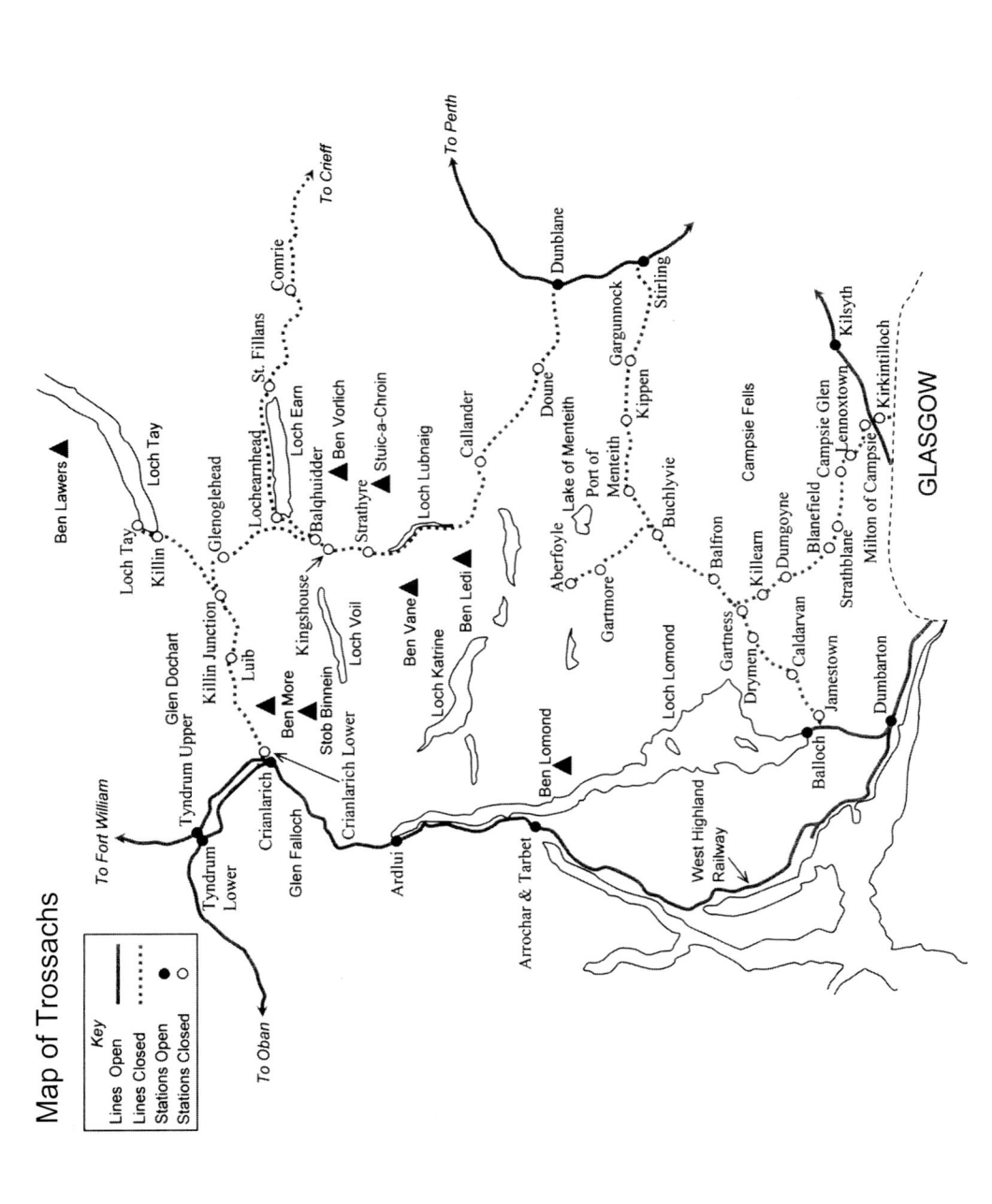

Chapter One

The Callander and Oban Railway

'One Man's Railway'

In a time of rapid railway expansion during the 1840s, the Scottish Central Railway (SCR), one of Scotland's pioneering railway companies, constructed a railway from Larbert to Perth via Stirling. Through agreements with other companies the SCR expanded their influence to Glasgow, Edinburgh, Aberdeen and Inverness and took over the failing Dundee and Perth Railway Company. The gap in the company portfolio was the west, and with tourism in the Trossachs beginning to develop, people wanted to visit but bad roads and poor stagecoach services prevented all but the most determined. The attraction of opening up the West Highlands to tourism and reaching fishing ports like Oban encouraged speculators to plan routes and seek backing. Out of this developed the plans which were to become in time the Callander and Oban Railway (C&OR).

A start to opening up the Trossachs to visitors had been made with the construction of the independent Dunblane, Doune and Callander Railway (DD&CR) in 1858. The eleven mile route was relatively easy to construct and linked with the SCR at Dunblane. North of Callander, however, firstly through narrow Perthshire valleys to reach Oban on the west coast, was not easy territory for railways either geographically or in business terms. Delivering the fish landed by the fishing fleets from the rich fishing grounds off the west coast, to the central belt and beyond was, however, one of the few potential sources of business. Even dreams of Oban as an Atlantic port were touted; this was after all the era of railway expansionism when any proposal was permissible, if it helped attract financial backing. The trains, it was suggested, could also ease the long and difficult journey of cattle to markets. Fish and cattle would, therefore, help compensate a railway company for the lack of people in the Western Highlands.

The SCR received the proposals, outlining a route from Oban along the shore of Loch Etive, through the Pass of Brander and by Dalmally to Crianlarich. At Crianlarich there was a choice of both south by Glen Falloch and then Loch Lomond or east by Glen Dochart and then south through Glen Ogle to Callander. Few railway companies were interested and the SCR was pitted against the relative lightweights of The Forth and Clyde and the Blane Valley Railways, who naturally favoured the Glen Falloch route to bring the railway close to their territory. The route to Callander led more easily to SCR territory and with its financial backing this proposal won the day. Five of the nine directors of the C&OR were to be appointed by the SCR who agreed to work it once twenty miles had been constructed and the route passed fit for use by the Board of Trade.

It was, however, a time of rapid change in the railway industry. Ten days before the Act of Parliament authorising the C&OR was passed, the SCR was allowed to take over the DD&CR from the 31st July 1865, giving them control of the rails to Callander. One day later, all changed, and the SCR was in turn absorbed by the Caledonian Railway (CR), who in turn acquired the obligation made by the SCR to the C&OR.

The CR viewed the Callander and Oban Railway with dismay – it would after all be expensive to construct. A major player like the CR didn't want to waste money when the coal fields of Lanarkshire and the links to Carlisle and Aberdeen were far more lucrative. Countering this was the natural suspicion that fuelled inter-company rivalries. Would the North British Railway Company (NBR) step in and exploit the rights they already had to traverse the rails to Callander? What if they made a success and opened up the West Highlands? After all, they had already penetrated CR country and reached the Clyde Coast. The CR had to be careful.

Local support for the C&OR was not sufficient to bridge the funding gap between the money committed by the CR and the total build costs. This raised hopes in the Caledonian boardroom that the railway link to Oban would never materialise and indeed would quietly fade away.

They would probably have been right, if it hadn't been for one remarkable man. John Anderson had gained experience with the Edinburgh and Glasgow Railway (E&GR), starting as a boy clerk at Falkirk where, by chance, he had operated the first telegraph in Scotland in the presence of the patent holder, Bain. He moved to the newly opened Waverley Station and then to Glasgow where he was the assistant to the General Superintendent. Afterwards he spent ten years as the assistant manager at the E&GR and the SCR. He fought and failed to prevent the take over of the Edinburgh and Glasgow by the NBR. On their merger in 1865 he accepted the post of secretary of the C&OR. He served different railway companies for a total of sixty-one years becoming manager of the C&OR when it eventually reached Oban fifteen years later. In this capacity he also oversaw the building of the Killin and Ballachulish branches for the C&OR. The new secretary, who accepted the poisoned chalice of a split boardroom, was both experienced and able to fight his own corner and that is what this project required. Anderson's problems were multiple: apart from a divided board, the majority hostile to the line being developed, there were limited funds and a challenging route through difficult terrain. He first set about ensuring that those who had subscribed 'paid-up.' This was not always easy, as some even denied having committed to buying any shares. Anderson scoured the land to raise funds, with no sum too small to interest him. A prodigious writer he penned around 20,000 letters in his attempts to extend and complete the railway.

A resourceful man, John Anderson was well suited to providing low cost solutions for a cash strapped railway. The danger of rock falls as the railway passed through rock strewn hill sides was a concern to the C&OR engineers and he invented a wire screen that operated signals if hit by a falling boulder. Anderson's Piano, as the system became known, due to the humming sound made by wind blowing through it, was successful in reducing the risk of an accident. A night-bell system was also installed for a cost of £75 ensuring that trains were not held up unnecessarily at night or by snow blocking the line. His influence was everywhere, even designing the ladies toilet doors, with clear instructions about the standard of painting and the gilt letters to be used. Despite all this, he still found time to be an enthusiastic gardener and photographer.

The appointed engineers, Blyth and Cunningham were made aware of the money problems and suggested an initial seventeen and a half mile section, as far as Glenogleheaad, be built. This was short of the twenty miles necessary to ensure that the CR committed to operate it, but Anderson recommended it to his board.

The first contract was obtained by John MacKay but delays meant that it was nearly the winter of 1866 before he could begin. Construction began between Callander and Lochearnhead with camps set up for the navvies. From Callander through the Pass of Leny progress was rapid and also from St Brides Crossing to Strathyre across almost level ground the trackbed was soon laid. Anderson had a difficult balancing act – if progress was too quick then there might not be sufficient funds to pay the contractor or local landowners. Some landowners were very difficult to deal with. This was particularly true of Sir Malcolm Macgregor of the Edinchip estate, south of Lochearnhead, who originally demanded a tunnel be built under his land but fortunately this was disallowed by parliament. The estate was missed out for as long as possible but when allowed to start, a watchful factor ensured no collateral damage. Rails arrived by the following summer but just when progress was being made, the CR faction on the board stopped all work for the year. This prevented the necessary preparation work for the next year being started. Anderson fought back; arguing that the decision would make fund raising even more difficult and eventually compromise was reached. MacKay eased the situation by accepting a token payment.

Difficult weather delayed matters further and fuelled sentiment for abandoning the project which went even as far as framing an 'Abandonment Bill.' While the C&OR shareholders were presented with a glowing report, the CR shareholders saw a terminus on a lonely and deserted hillside. The latter view was more objective but Anderson would not give up. The railway brought benefits and Anderson was keen to highlight this to the locals through schemes such as arranging for cheaper coal to be delivered to the residents of Strathyre, winning their hearts. Anderson also encouraged locals to be involved and ensured that they could make a contribution. The people of Kingshouse, between Strathyre and Lochearnhead, at the head of Balquhidder Glen, petitioned for a platform for their community, which he agreed, as long as they built it themselves. It was added in June 1871.

Beyond the site of Lochearnhead Station (later Balquhidder Station) the going became tougher with the entry into Glen Ogle and an almost continuous gradient of one in sixty. A narrow ledge high on the hillside had to be blasted out of the hard rock to reach Glenoglehead, where Killin Station was to be sited 941 feet above sea level and three and a half miles from the small village at the western end of Loch Tay. Costs restricted the plans for the stations. Callander and Killin were basic wooden structures; Strathyre and Lochearnhead consisted only of a booking office and a porter's lodge. Other necessities like engine sheds were just as basic.

Surprisingly it was only in May, with the opening scheduled for 1st June 1870, that Anderson made final arrangements for the use of CR engines. Two trains a day were all that he could afford. Recognising that on arrival at Killin passengers were being deposited in the middle of nowhere, Anderson arranged for local transport to link with the trains.

Anderson was shrewd highlighting the scenic attractions of the railway; Glen Ogle was described as the equivalent of the Khyber Pass but he also ensured coach links to Luib, Ballachulish and Oban – pointing in the direction that the railway was to take. He devoted a lot of time to encouraging special excursions from the central belt eventually getting the CR to offer special excursion tickets, for the C&OR, from many stations. Even hill guides were organised by Anderson to ensure that visitors could explore the countryside after their trip on the C&OR. With the end of summer, the line became a lot quieter with the short tourist season ending. Enough money had to be earned during the summer to keep the line going and pay a dividend. It was hard work and would have demoralised a less committed person. However, the railway was surviving and by 1871 was being extended to Tyndrum, an additional 17 miles. This involved a descent from Glenoglehead as the line turned west along the southern edge of Glen Dochart, passing through Luib to reach Crianlarich. From Crianlarich the route turned north-west to reach Tyndrum. Work was completed by August 1873. Just under half-way, Anderson must have been pleased and immediately set out to establish contacts with coach operators and boat operators. Tourists were enticed from the Firth of Clyde to Arrochar and Ardrishaig piers and coached to Crianlarich and Tyndrum where they joined a train tour.

The CR was not helpful in providing trains for the regular timetable. Two trains a day from Tyndrum at 5.30am and 2pm did little to encourage people to use the train. As usual Anderson fought his corner to ensure fairness.

By now the CR, despite poor traffic results, decided to 'bite the bullet' and complete the route to Oban. Their shareholders, experiencing at that time rising dividends, increased stock value and improving traffic revenue, did not object.

Another 12 miles were completed, then more capital was injected from an English railway company, the London and North-Western Railway (L&NWR) and the final difficult terrain was crossed. The route kept to the shores of Loch Awe, round Ben Cruachan and through the narrow Pass of Brander. Bridges and many twists and turns were required to reach the shores of Loch Etive. Here the railway was forced to turn inland to reach Oban. The welcome from Oban was however mixed. The railway's chosen route spoiled the view on the sea front. Others saw advantages with the railway's plans allowing easier access to steamers. A compromise was reached and by 1st July 1870 the line was opened. To the conqueror came the spoils. His contribution was finally acknowledged. John Anderson was made company secretary and traffic manager. He moved to Oban and stayed there for another twenty-seven years. On the ceremonial opening the town turned out to toast the railway's arrival – past tensions forgotten.

On the 125th anniversary of the arrival of the railway in Oban, in 2005, a commemorative plaque was unveiled in the new Oban station. It simply states: 'Honouring John Anderson, 1837-1911, without whom the railway would not have been completed.' The plaque offers a fitting epitaph to a remarkable railway entrepreneur.

Exploring the Railway Heritage

All the routes in this chapter are covered by the following maps: Explorer 364, 365, 366. There are also several good local maps in this popular tourist area describing walks and cycle routes along parts of the trackbed.

While the Callander and Oban Railway begins at Callander, without the Dunblane, Doune and Callander Railway it would never have existed and an exploration of the heritage left by the DD&CR is included. Trains still run on the original C&OR route west of Crianlarich and so this chapter concentrates on the disused section from Dunblane to Crianlarich. Do plan, however, to enjoy the train journey on to Oban from Crianlarich.

The exploration is split into four parts; Dunblane to Callander, Callander to Balquhidder, Balquhidder to Glenoglehead and Glenoglehead to Crianlarich. Bus services are limited and should be carefully checked out. In winter the last three sections can be very demanding and proper walking equipment and due care is required. The section from Callander to Glen Ogle is both part of the Rob Roy Way (a long distance walking path starting in Drymen and ending at Pitlochry) and part of the National Cycle Route no 7.

There were stations at Doune (4 miles from Dunblane), Callander (11 miles), Strathyre (20 miles), Kingshouse (22 miles), Balquhidder (23 miles), Glenoglehead Crossing (formerly Killin) (29 miles), Killin Junction (32 miles), Luib (34 miles) and Crianlarich Junction (40 miles).

Dunblane to Callander

Only the section from west of the A9 to Doune is walkable. The DD&CR branched from the Stirling to Perth line in Dunblane, a town with a famous ancient cathedral originally founded by St Blane. Situated five miles north of Stirling the railway plays an important role in the life of the town allowing commuters to travel to Glasgow and Edinburgh. The station at Dunblane, with its three platforms is still in use, and retains many of the original buildings and features such as the crow-stepped gables on the station offices. The enclosed footbridge to the island platform has been retained and a new footbridge has been added to allow locals to cross the station site. From another footbridge north of the station, accessed from Caledonian Place, close to Tesco supermarket, there is a good viewpoint of the junction site (780012) and the Dunblane signalbox. The cathedral tower can also be seen to the north-east. The DD&CR branched from the Stirling to Perth railway line just north of the footbridge on the opposite side of the track from a signal box. Nowadays all that remains of the line is a short siding, which is no longer in use and is very overgrown. On the far side of the buffers, housing development obscures the route through Dunblane with only a couple of over bridges, with their rusting plate metal sides remaining, to show the direction taken by the line. The A9 trunk road which now bypasses the town to the west provides a further obstacle to exploration. After crossing over the A9, using the A820, the trackbed can be rediscovered by taking the first minor road to the right leading to Stockbridge Farm.

The trackbed can then be followed west through farmland being found where the road crosses it. The minor road loops round and eventually rejoins the A820. In the process the railway crosses over it by a brick lined single arch bridge, near Auchenteck Farm. However, the next rail bridge over the Ardoch Burn has been demolished with one concrete abutment left. This obstacle can be bypassed by following the minor road close to its junction with the A820. Here a path leads to the trackbed, which is used as a nature trail all the way into Doune. The first section between Dunblane and Doune was made double track by 1901 because the route was so busy. The trackbed is crossed by two road bridges before a replacement wooden bridge crosses a small burn. Through a succession of cuttings and embankments, the railway builders smoothed out the land on the approach to Doune. The attractive village with its prominent church towers is quickly reached, with the railway crossing a minor road before passing under a road bridge to reach the site of Doune Station.

At the same time as the track was doubled, the station was redeveloped with the intention of turning the village into a commuter town. The new station was very grand for such a small community and some thought that this was due to the General Manager and later Chairman of the CR, Sir James Thompson living close by! The station at Doune (725018) consisted of an island platform with a hip-roofed wooden building, constructed on a stone base. To each side of the building were elaborate ridged glass canopies, reaching to the edges of the platforms. An enclosed footbridge linked the station to the village. A further footbridge allowed access from the village to sand and gravel quarries on the other side of the railway, with the quarry machinery prominent beside the station for many years. The nearby Doune Ponds, now a nature reserve, are reclaimed from these sand and gravel quarries. Platform edging slabs are the only remnant of the station and with housing planned for the area the edging slabs will also disappear. Already the houses in Cadell Loan have been built over the former site of the main station buildings. The station house (listed category B) however remains at the entrance to Station Wynd.

Doune is a village situated by the River Teith, where the Ardoch Burn joins it close to Doune Castle. It is closely linked with Deanston village, where there was a cotton mill, whose premises are now used to produce whisky. The well preserved Doune Castle, to the east of the village, is protected on two sides by the river and the third by a deep moat. If it appears familiar it is probably because it was used as the backdrop to the 1975 film *Monty Python and the Holy Grail*. The village was also once famous for the manufacture of pistols, a skill introduced by Thomas Cadell in the seventeenth century. His pistols were involved in the first shots fired in the American War of Independence. Cadell has also had an indirect influence in the demise of the railway as both 'Thomas Cadell Loan' and 'Pistolmakers Row' are built over sections of the railway station site.

Sadly, the next section of the DD&CR between Doune and the Bridge of Keltie Camping Site is not suitable for walking although there are plans to open a cycle path along the former railway. The first section to Drumvaich signal box, where there was a passing loop, is very overgrown and there are several missing bridges. The signal box and house have been redeveloped as an attractive private residence. Beyond Drumvaich the trackbed is blocked by quarries which continue as far as a camp site with the trackbed being used as an access road. The final mile into Callander begins at the Bridge of Keltie. A single span stone bridge over the Keltie Water leads to the Bridge of Keltie Camping Site. A path extends through a former quarry up to where the

Doune looking to Stirling 1956

trackbed can be rejoined closer to Callander, behind housing. Over the tops of the modern houses is the view, familiar to many who travelled by train, of the towering Ben Ledi, an indication that the terrain is about to change. At 2875 feet it is not quite a Munro but still effortlessly dominates Callander.

The road bridge which crosses over the former railway and leads to the beautiful Bracklinn Falls, in the hills above Callander, is still intact, with alterations to the trackbed reducing the headroom. Cyclists do not require as much height as trains. The original terminus of the DD&CR was located just before the road bridge but nothing remains. Twelve years after the line was opened the railway was extended from Callander Junction to the 'new' Callander Station further west and the section between the two stations was made double track in 1903. Closed for passengers, shortly after the C&OR station was opened, the site remained in use as a goods depot until 1965. However there was a 'ticket platform' at the old station for use at busy times, when thousands of people could arrive maybe as part of a company day out. Tickets were checked and the train then continued to the station where passengers could disembark more quickly. There was another 'ticket platform' at Oban.

From the road bridge more detours are required, due to house building, but the direction of the track can still be followed with enough remnants of the railway remaining – mainly stone work. Eventually Station Road is reached which winds up and over the former railway. To the left are houses, again built on the line, but to the right is a large car park, the site of the C&OR Callander Station (626083). The station was built on a curve between the town and the steep, thickly wooded hillside. There were two signal boxes. The East Box was located at the Dunblane end, near the bridge and the West Box at the Oban

Callander ticket platform (blurred photograph included for historical interest)

Callander looking to Doune 1965

end. The main station building, with steeply pitched roofs, was on a wide platform with an extra bay. It was located behind the Dreadnought Hotel and the station was officially known as Callander Dreadnought until the 1930s. Opposite the main building, linked by a footbridge, was a narrower platform with a further station building. Avoiding lines ran behind this platform and the hillside.

The station was also the first stop for the 'Six Lochs Land Cruise' which started from Glasgow (Buchanan Street). The rail tour was extremely successful, after the Second World War, visiting Loch Lubnaig, Loch Earn, Loch Tay, Loch Lomond, Loch Long and Gareloch.

Devotees of the original *Dr Finlay's Casebook,* written by A.J.Cronin, will know that Callander was used as the setting of the fictional Tannochbrae and brought many tourists to the area. Arden House, the doctor's home was located on the road to Bracklinn Falls. The railway station used in the filming of the popular 1960s BBC series however, was not Callander but Uplawmoor Station (formerly Caldwell Station) on the Glasgow Barrhead and Kilmarnock line which was renamed Tannochbrae for the occasion.

Uplawmoor - temporarily renamed - 1966

Callander to Balquhidder

The nine mile stretch from Callander to Strathyre is part of the Rob Roy Way and National Cycle Route No.7. The trackbed is in good condition. Shorter walks could start from Bochastle Hill next to the A821 (1 mile from Callander (608081)) or the Ben Ledi car park accessed by a bridge over the River Teith north of the Falls of Leny (3 miles from Callander (586092)). From Strathyre to Balquhidder the trackbed is not easy to follow and runs beside a busy road. Alternatives are to use the cycle route, clearly signposted from Strathyre or miss out the section.

Passengers waiting to travel on to Oban would soon notice a difference from their carriage window as the big hills closed in and the valleys narrowed. After a few miles, the gradient would rise and the travellers would be transported into the Highlands. Callander located on the edge of the fertile lowlands would soon be left behind and John Anderson's 'Khyber Pass' would be entered, a different world filled with a stark beauty and striking atmosphere.

After Callander Station the railway once passed under the A84, but this next short section has been removed. Railway signal posts indicate the start of the popular Callander to Strathyre cycle route. The trackbed cuts across the floodplain of the River Teith, crossing the river by a new bridge and passing the remains of a Roman fort. The Romans were not keen to explore north of here and may have been intimidated by the approaching hills and the risk of being ambushed. The trackbed then crosses the A821 Trossachs road, on the level. The road has being rerouted to bypass the original road bridge over the line, which still exists, before starting the long climb, at a gradient of one in sixty, towards the Pass of Leny. Surrounded by trees that must have once muffled the sound of labouring engines, nowadays only the sound of road traffic from across the valley and the whoosh of passing cyclists disturb the tranquillity at the start of the walk. Oak trees in the woods were once used as a source of charcoal for local iron smelting. As the climb continues the roar of water funnelled through the narrow Pass of Leny becomes louder as the Falls of Leny, spectacular in full spate after heavy rain, are reached. Here the railway crossed the river not once but twice, by narrow single span bowstring girder bridges. Only the bricked off abutments remain and the cycle path provides a detour leading to the car park for the climbers to leave their cars to climb Ben Ledi.

The next section provided a relief for the steam trains as it is very flat. Known as St Brides Crossing, there is a ruined chapel of the same name on the other side of the loch. The trackbed now doubles as an access road to the holiday chalets a short distance ahead. John Anderson had hoped to open a station here but met a rare rebuff when his plans were blocked by the local landowner. He did manage, however, to build a signal box to control the single track loop. This section once won a prize for being the best maintained mile of track — after the Falls of Leny section it must have been a pleasure to maintain. There are views ahead towards the imposing and distinctive Ben Vorlich. To the right Loch Lubnaig starts to widen.

Beyond the holiday chalets the steep hillside to the west closes in on the track leaving a narrow passage for the trackbed between the hill and the loch. Rock Cottages are reached perched on a ridge overlooking a cutting. This was the site of Craig-nan-Cailleach (Rock of the old woman) Halt (583123). A path once led down from the cottage to a platform made up of railway

Craig-nan-Cailleach platform 1961

sleepers. At 8.35am, much to the chagrin of some passengers, the Oban to Callander express was stopped to allow pupils to go to school in Callander. In the evening the process was reversed and initially by travelling in the brake van of a goods train and then using a shunting engine pulling two carriages the scholars were returned to destinations all the way up the valley. There are steep cliff faces behind the former halt and large boulders lying by the trackside suggested that Anderson was right to be concerned about rock falls. A train would be destroyed by one of the large boulders. His piano wire system was installed on the high cliff faces and, if tripped, would sound a loud bell in the cottages at the halt. The protective wires were even mentioned in a 1960s advertising booklet as a 'feature of interest'. It is not clear how reassuring this was to passengers.

Rumours persist of an engine derailed when the line was being constructed and lurking under the surface of Loch Lubnaig near Rock Cottages. In certain conditions it may even be visible. Strangely, this far into CR territory, some believe that it was a North British engine. In 1972 a diver searched for the engine but could not continue due to the number of cars, vans and caravans dumped since the line closed. Shortly after Rock Cottages the trackbed deviates from the former railway climbing to provide views over the loch. Follow the cycle route and enjoy the views. The railway track is rejoined near Laggan Farm. Another platform was provided here by the railway. From here to Strathyre there are several over bridges with only the abutments remaining.

The last stretch of trackbed on the approach to Strathyre is blocked, a conservation area, and walkers are directed by the signposted cycle route which leads through forestry homes to a suspension bridge over the River Balvag. This replaces the railway bridge as does the next bridge. Between the two bridges there is an alternative route into the village. Continuing over the second bridge a tarmac path leads behind recently built houses. It was here that Strathyre Station (560171) was located. House building has removed the station site. Initially there was only one platform, a loop and short siding. Over time as business improved a second platform was added and a goods shed constructed. Sidings fanned out into the space now immediately in front of the village store. Apparent in many photographs of the station was a fountain in the shape of a heron on a granite plinth. The heron fountain was the reward chosen by the station master at Strathyre, John Robertson Sutherland, in recognition of his forty-one years service and for winning the best-kept station award on numerous occasions. The heron was 'rescued' when

Strathyre Heron

the station closed, and now resides in the front lawn of a nearby house, on the opposite side of the A84. The plinth reads: 'Cruachan granite' and the heron has since aquired a coat of paint. The station was rebuilt after a fire in 1893. The wooden structures, deemed necessary by Anderson's economies were more vulnerable to fire. The railway continued, passing under a minor road, but the cycle route uses this minor road to reach Balquhidder. The bridge has been infilled. Strathyre is a busy village in summer and being trapped between wooded hillsides in a narrow valley it offers a good starting point to many of the nearby hills and to fishing on Loch Lubnaig. The railway trackbed between Strathyre Station and Kingshouse Halt is located between the winding River Balvag and the A84. This part of the valley is prone to flooding so the trackbed was constructed closer to the road on higher ground. Some parts of the trackbed are lost to farming and near Kingshouse to road realignment. The A84 is a very busy route and you are advised to miss out this section.

The cycle route deviates from the trackbed at Strathyre to take in the head of Balquhidder Glen and Balquhidder village. This is an on-road section of the cycle route. The detour is longer but worthwhile as it leads into Balquhidder Glen before winding back out to the A84. The grave of Rob Roy at Balquhidder Church and the beautiful Kirkton Glen are worth a visit. From Kirkton Glen it's possible to walk over the hills to Ledcharrie Farm, near Luib, crossing the C&OR trackbed as it passes through Glen Dochart to the north.

Balquhidder Glen is one of those special places best described by an old Gaelic saying that there are 'some places where the veil between heaven and earth is thin'. The glen has stunning scenery with the attractions of Loch Voil and Loch Doine surrounded by hills and further valleys. With its connections to Rob Roy, Balquhidder has a strong sense of history and an amazing feeling of peace and tranquillity. I imagine that the sound of the steam trains climbing from Strathyre to Lochearnhead and beyond would have echoed along the glen, a consoling sound, suggesting a bond between the many small communities and a reassuring link with the outside world. The schoolchildren using the train to return from school in Callander were about to re-enter a magical place. Tourists with time to spare can investigate the haunting beauty but in contrast the trucks travelling along the A84 barely seem to notice the hills and glens, busy trying to reach their destinations.

The A84 now bypasses Kingshouse with its historic hotel. Just before the cycle route leaves the glen, it passes under the realigned A84. Immediately to the south, on an overgrown embankment, was Kingshouse Halt (563203). Nothing remains of it. The cycle route diverges from the road immediately before it passes under the A84. It continues north, through woodland, before emerging opposite the site of Balquhidder Station. This is a much easier

Kingshouse platform looking north

route to take than trying to trace the remnants of the old railway between Kingshouse and the next station on the line at Balquhidder.

Balquhidder Station to Glenoglehead

The 6.5 miles from Balquhidder Station to Glenoglehead is part of the Rob Roy Way and National Cycle Route No.7. The trackbed is in good condition. The first two miles uses the trackbed of the former Lochearnhead, St. Fillans and Comrie Railway (LSF&CR) before a steep connecting path links to the C&OR trackbed higher up the hillside. The LSF&CR passes through the village of Lochearnhead and then turns east along the northern shore of Loch Earn. The C&OR continues to climb above Lochearnhead and through Glen Ogle to reach Glenoglehead.

From Glenoglehead, there is an infrequent bus service but a convenient car park close by on the opposite side of the road to leave your car. The journey could be continued to Killin Junction – start of Killin Railway (KR) and either down to the A85 near Lix Toll, or onto Killin itself (described in the chapter on the Killin Railway)

Balquhidder station site, the crossing of the Edinchip Viaduct and the section to the connecting path between the two railways is described in the section on the Comrie Railway in Chapter Two. While not part of the Rob Roy Way, the Callander and Oban route can also be traced from Balquhidder station but it is not a recognised path and gates may be locked.

Start of the walk using the Callander and Oban trackbed from Balquhidder Station.

From the Balquhidder Braes Caravan Park, which is the site of Balquhidder Station (574210) the C&OR crossed over the road by a bridge. The road has been realigned and traces of the bridge removed. The trackbed climbs away from the missing bridge on an embankment which is now tree lined. To the right beside the road are railway cottages. There are a couple of missing bridges, which make for a scramble before a high fence is reached. If the gate is open, then the journey can be continued. If locked, then a short detour is required and the Rob Roy Way can be picked up heading towards Lochearnhead along the former Comrie Railway trackbed (National Cycle Route No.7).

The C&OR trackbed is used as an access road and crosses the old military road before emerging from woods. It then climbs towards more trees. On the approach to the trees is a four arch viaduct which crosses the Kendrum Burn near a waterfall. Further downhill the Comrie Railway crossed the same burn by the more spectacular Edinchip or Kendrum Viaduct. The views are spectacular. South-east, across the valley, is Stuc a' Chroin and slightly further north is Ben Vorlich. South is the heavily wooded Strathyre valley and to the south-west the start of Balquhidder Glen. To the west the hills tower over the trackbed. This is dramatic railway landscape and before the trees were planted must have been even more rugged with stone strewn hillsides and for locomotives, at a gradient of one in sixty for six miles, a challenging struggle. This section of the C&OR crosses the Edinchip estate, whose owner once proved so awkward to John Anderson. A short distance from the viaduct is

Balquhidder looking south 1950

one of the concessions wrung from the railway – an elaborate access bridge to the upper hills. The bridge consists of a single wrought iron arch with wooden decking and decorative cross-members supported by masonry abutments.

As the climb continues, Edinchip Farm is seen downhill. Further minor rail bridges and over bridges confirm that this was not an easy route to construct. The continued climb exposes more views as the line veers north-west. To the east is Loch Earn and at the head of the loch below the trackbed is the village of Lochearnhead. High hills fringe the north and south edges of this beautiful loch, which runs east towards St Fillans. Some train enthusiasts have described this as the most impressive railway vista in Britain. The railway towards Comrie crossed the glen below by the Lochearnhead Viaduct; its concrete structure can still be seen.

Continuation of the walk from where the national cycle path joins the trackbed of the Callander and Oban

The C&OR route then becomes part of the national cycle way as a short and steep connecting path, with its steep ramp and hairpin bends, links the Comrie Railway trackbed with the Callander and Oban (584239). From here the route can be continued to Glenoglehead, or following the path down to the former Comrie railway you can walk back to the site of Balquhidder Station, a short but interesting circular walk. It is also possible to use this path to reach Lochearnhead. Further on, there is another steep and difficult path which leads down to the Lochearnhead Station site. Beyond that the walker is committed to continuing to Glenoglehead or turning back because the hillside

View from north-bound train near Glenoglehead 1950

is too steep to scramble down. The trackbed is a narrow ridge hacked out of the hillside and enters Glen Ogle, a narrow steep sided valley, through which the Ogle Burn runs. On the eastern side is the A85 and in the depths of the valley is the old military road. Glen Ogle was, not surprisingly, one of the few sections of the line which could get blocked when the snow came. The line clings to the western slopes of the glen, receiving little direct sunshine in the winter. With a sufficient covering of snow, the snow could become unstable and cascade down the steep slopes onto the railway. Morning is also the best time to photograph this stretch of railway, since the west side of the valley is soon in shade.

The landslide which closed the C&OR, on Monday 27 September 1965, partially covered the line just above Glenogle Farm. Only one rail was covered and this led to much cynical speculation in the local press that British Railways Board was using the landslide as an excuse to close the line five weeks before it was planned. Reality was that the landslide was more extensive and left the hillside unstable with further rock falls liable at any time. The railway engineers were annoyed with the negative press they received. It has to be said, however, that in the intervening years no further landslide has occurred and that SUSTRANS and Stirling Council must believe that it is safe, having invested in a substantial upgrade to the trackbed to become a cycle route. From the trackbed of the C&OR there are further good views of the Lochearnhead Viaduct on the disused Comrie route. As the views of Loch Earn become more restricted the site of another landslide can be seen on the road side of the valley. A landslip caused by heavy rain, blocked the road trapping cars. Eventually, and with urgency, the road was cleared, unlike the railway! The road threads round outcrops of rock making for difficult and demanding bends. It is a dangerous road and by opening up the old railway track a safe option has been provided for cyclists and walkers.

Landslide blocking Callander and Oban Railway 1965

There are many minor rail bridges crossing the numerous burns which cascade down the hillside. Frequently the railway builders must have been working in poor weather; one can only admire the tenacity of those who

30

laboured in demanding conditions creating a route which must have scarred the hillside with rocky obstacles blasted to make way for the railway. Retaining walls and stone channels to direct the water under the track were frequently required. Trees, mainly larch with some rowan, have sprouted along the sides of the trackbed giving a more benign look.

One feature which draws admiration from drivers on the road is the iconic Glen Ogle Viaduct (571263). The twelve arch masonry viaduct crosses a basin in the hillside, curving inwards. The trackbed is now tarmacked at this point and the stone parapet has a sturdy metal fence which is important if you want to lean over to get a clear picture of the viaduct. The best view is from the road. This truly was John Anderson's Khyber Pass.

Near the summit the route enters a cutting crossed by a stone overbridge. Considerable work has been carried out to ensure that the drainage is working. Don't be surprised to see a land rover parked by the side as the rangers carry out maintenance along the length of the track. Gates ensure boy racers cannot use the route. There has been a lot of investment in this section made possible because all the bridges and viaducts were of stone construction. Metal spans tend to be removed quickly on closure for scrap.

The summit is reached near Lochan Larig Eala, now surrounded almost completely by trees, which was the source of water for the steam locomotives in this section. The Lochan is named on the present map as Lochan Lairig Cheile. The trackbed is in touching distance of the road, brought together by the narrowing confines of the valley. Here is the site of the original Killin Station (558285). Without the trees, it must have been very bleak. No wonder the Caledonian shareholders had their doubts – the station was in the middle of nowhere! Opposite the station site, on the far side of the road, is now the

Glen Ogle Viaduct today - now a cycle path

Glen Ogle car park and the continuation of the cycle route, which leads down to Killin and joins the KR trackbed for a short distance. A well-known stopping place, there is usually a van selling coffee and snacks. A short distance along the cycle track is a memorial stone for two pilots, flight lieutenants Patrick Harrison and Peter Mosley, killed when their Tornado fighter plane crashed nearby in September 1994.

The station platforms remain and on the right a brick building. The station buildings, now converted and extended into two cottages are between the former railway and the road. There was a passing loop at the station. At 941 feet, this was the summit of the line – the end of a long climb. The station was renamed Glenoglehead in April 1886 when the KR opened and then Glenoglehead Crossing in September 1891. It only survived as a passenger station for three years and after that time passengers intending to disembark had to inform the guard at Balquhidder or Killin Junction. Until 1916 passengers could be dropped off if they were travelling on the early morning mail train and only then if the train was carrying mail. After 1916 only railway workers could use it and it became a private halt.

Glenoglehead to Crianlarich

This is a journey of 11 miles – The single metal span of Luib Viaduct is missing, (the stream is fordable in very dry weather). Beyond Luib there are only short sections of the trackbed walkable due to road realignment. Conditions underfoot are not easy beyond Luib and the A85 is very busy. Plan to walk back from Luib or connect with a bus onto your destination! Check bus times carefully, the service is not good.

The section between Glenoglehead and Killin Junction is now an access road for the forestry. The gradient decreases at a steady rate but that of the nearby road even faster creating the illusion that the trackbed is still climbing. The route curves north-west and then almost due west. The forest blocks most views but ahead lie the prominent peaks of Ben More and to the south Stob Binnein. Gradually as the forest is felled the views, which must have entranced railway travellers, will be restored. Killin Junction is found in a clearance in the forest. It is described in the chapter on the Killin Railway, where it belongs, but the C&OR would have disputed this as they made it clear to the KR that it belonged to them.

Beyond the station site the forest is soon left behind and the views mostly restored. The three arch stone Ardchyle Viaduct is crossed and also the three arch Ledcharrie Viaduct. In the chapter on the KR this is suggested as a good starting point to explore the Killin railway. A path leads up from the A85 and can be used to reach the trackbed. This path also continues over the hills into Balquhidder Glen.

Luib Viaduct abutments

    The trackbed has now entered into Glen Dochart and the route cuts across a more gently sloping hillside with sheep grazing on the lower slopes. The valley is wider and the River Dochart meanders alongside the A85. The gentler slopes do give way to rocky outcrops and higher peaks but the surroundings are not as dominating or as oppressive as in Glen Ogle. Travelling west, a wooden hut is located beside a metal gate with a swinging side gate to permit access to the railway. The gate is original and probably the hut was linked to the railway. The trackbed is lined with trees and passes through a shallow cutting. Luib Viaduct consisted of a single metal span with masonry abutments. Only the abutments remain. Cobbled stones line the bottom of the stream, which could be crossed in very dry weather. In wet weather a long detour to the nearby road would be required.

    On the west side of Luib Viaduct, (this was during a dry spell), the trackbed continues towards Luib Station generally by shallow tree lined cuttings or low embankments. After Glen Ogle this was easy to construct. It is almost five miles since Glenoglehead Crossing but the approach to Luib Station (479280) is like a return to civilisation. However, Luib once consisted only of an inn used by drovers bringing their cattle to the markets in the central belt. Even today, few people live in the vicinity of the station and most of these are temporary residents since the station site is now occupied by the expanding Glen Dochart Caravan Park. The usual attraction of good drainage and level surface associated with railway station sites is ideal for caravans. The original station cottage remains, but the wooden building on the southern side has been removed. The concrete edged platforms have been filled in and are occupied by a camp site, part of the caravan park. Opposite the station cottages there

Luib looking east 1956

is a sheep creep and the concrete edge of a platform. There was a siding to the north, facing east and a water tower. The base of the water tower has been preserved and now has a new wooden pointed roof. The now demolished signal box was to the west of the water tower and to the right of the track.

This was an isolated station which must have generated very little local business. Seasonal sheep and cattle trains to markets may have been arranged but so few people lived in the area that the number of passengers embarking or disembarking must have been low. The water tower gives one hint of why the station existed. The station, however, closed only with the rest of the line and the station site is now busier than it ever was.

Base of water tower, Luib Station site

West of Luib Station

The condition of the trackbed deteriorates and road realignment ensures the virtual disappearance of the route from Loch Lubhair to just east of Loch Dochart. The A85 is not a good road to walk beside given that traffic generally moves fast. Arrange transport or retrace your steps. To complete the journey a brief outline is given. From Luib Station the trackbed drops to the level of the road, having to cross it several times between here and Crianlarich. For the first mile the trackbed is found close to the River Dochart and to the north of the road. The route is lined with trees with only cattle for company but conditions underfoot can be difficult. A three arched masonry viaduct, with a bulging and unstable side, crosses the Allt Coire Chaorach Burn. The trackbed then enters a deep cutting next to a minor road leading to Auchessan Farm with conditions again difficult. The trackbed can be rediscovered, almost three miles west, near to Benmore Farm (413267), on the north side of the A85 and continues between the road and Loch Dochart until the outskirts of Crianlarich. While not a recognised walkway this is a picturesque section, with a ruined castle on an island in the middle of the loch. From some angles the ruins of the castle, consisting partly of a large chimney, looks like the pier of a viaduct, or may be it is just fatigue after a long walk! Screened by trees, most travellers on the A85 will miss this view. The castle was built by 'Black' Duncan Campbell of Glenorchy and was destroyed by the McNabs, who owned lands to the east, at the beginning of the seventeenth century.

The Crianlarich 'Link'

Crianlarich dominated by the towering Ben More to the south is situated where Glen Falloch meets Strath Fillan and is considered by many to be the gateway to the Western Highlands. The C&OR station was a simple wooden building with a canopy built over the platform. The canopy with a central line of pillars supporting it looked like a late addition to protect passengers from the frequent showers. The station has been demolished and houses built on the site. It was known as Crianlarich Lower (387253) after the opening of the West Highland line.

While the C&OR route linked to central Scotland, passengers travelling onto Glasgow had to go via Stirling which added about twenty miles. There had been speculation for some time about a direct route down Glen Falloch eventually linking up with the railway network near Glasgow, something indeed that the C&OR had considered themselves and the Glen Falloch route was the one selected by the West Highland Railway (WHR). Opened in 1894, the WHR left the existing NBR route, with its direct connections to Glasgow, at Craigendoran near Helensburgh. It passed along the eastern edge of Loch Long and continued between the neighbouring villages of Arrochar and Tarbet and along the western edge of Loch Lomond and through Glen Falloch to reach Crianlarich. It continued through Tyndrum and across Rannoch Moor to reach Fort William. The railway was operated by the NBR meaning that the two great railway rivals, the North British and the Caledonian were again facing up to each other.

Both Crianlarich and Tyndrum, small Highland villages, had two stations, one provided by the C&OR and the other by the WHR. The NBR route passed over the C&OR and the nearby River Fillan, at Crianlarich by the Glenbruar Viaduct, a steel truss structure on slim masonry piers. To the general public a connection between the two railways at Crianlarich was common sense. For the C&OR this was a problem. They stood to lose traffic as they feared, rightly, that people would choose the shorter route to Glasgow by the WHR rather than continue to Stirling. A spur was authorised by the 1889 Act, which diverged from the WHR route and ran west to link with the C&OR. It did not pass through the C&OR station, which was isolated about 800 yards to the east. This link is still in use today.

The C&OR had also entered into a prior agreement that the NBR would not have operating rights to Oban or indeed the C&OR to Fort William but carriages could be exchanged at Crianlarich. A clause in the bill also gave the C&OR a veto if they were not pleased with any modifications. A joint station was rejected by the them, as they did not wish two stations within 800 yards. The companies could not reach an agreement and went to arbitration with the outcome that the spur be built, without any platforms, with the WHR paying the costs. The NBR, who also had to pay to work the junction and provide a locomotive now decided not to operate the link since they still couldn't run their trains through to Oban. They also realised, however, that the C&OR could divert livestock traffic from Fort William to Stirling and Perth where there were big cattle markets.

It was not until December 1897 that the spur was opened but it was simply used for non passenger traffic. Only, in 1931, after the reorganisation of the railway network, when the WHR had been absorbed into the LNER and the C&OR into the LMS, was the spur eventually used for passenger traffic. Use was made for special excursions but only after nationalisation, a Glasgow (Queen Street) to Oban service was introduced. In the post-Beeching era two railway routes were unsustainable and the 'spur' favoured the original WHR route which gave access to Oban and didn't require reversing at Crianlarich. East of Crianlarich was prepared for closure which was brought forward by the Glen Ogle landslide. By chance, the Royal family were almost the last people to use the Crianlarich Lower Station when they slept in their carriage, waiting for the opening of the Ben Cruachan hydro-electric scheme. Crianlarich Lower found use as a loading point for timber bound for the pulp mill at Fort William and the revenue generated probably ensured that the WHR route remained open. Today the section from the site of Crianlarich Lower to the spur is largely overgrown with only a short siding being retained for storing trains.

Crianlarich Upper Station (385251) on the WHR line is now simply known as Crianlarich. The station was built where the road and railway emerge from the northern end of Glen Falloch and overlooks Strath Fillan. The station consists of an island platform, with a passenger subway from the road leading up to the platform. The station buildings to the south of the platform have been rebuilt after a fire. The older buildings at the northern end are originals and house a well-known 'tearoom', frequented by both thirsty rail travellers and walkers. Sidings to each side store timber for onward transportation. There is also the engine shed now used by civil engineers. A short distance north of the station is Crianlarich Junction where the route to Oban veers left, down the infamous spur, and the former WHR route continues over the Glenbruar Viaduct, closely followed by the Fillan Viaduct over the River Fillan.

The Crianlarich spur had a significant impact on the railways in the area. If the two companies could have compromised, a joint station would have benefited both routes but it would have remained unlikely that both of the routes would have remained open. Even today the 'spur' has an impact on Crianlarich creating an awkward and twisting corner on the A82 to the west of Crianlarich. Once the line was closed there was little delay in uplifting the line. Within three years the railway track had been exported to Mexico for use in the 1968 Olympics to provide a link between the athletes' village and the games.

What would John Anderson have made of the loss of twenty-nine miles of his beloved railway from Callander to Crianlarich? His hard work and determination have come to naught but the images of trains crossing the Falls of Leny, climbing Glen Ogle, or approaching Crianlarich remain as treasured railway memories. Some things cannot be erased.

Many a cyclist using the cycle track and arriving breathless at Glenoglehead will marvel at the thought of a steam train having made the climb up Glen Ogle. Anderson's achievements remain impressive: his single mindedness turned his dream into reality and even now you can always catch the train at Crianlarich and continue the journey along his route to Oban.

Map of West Highlands

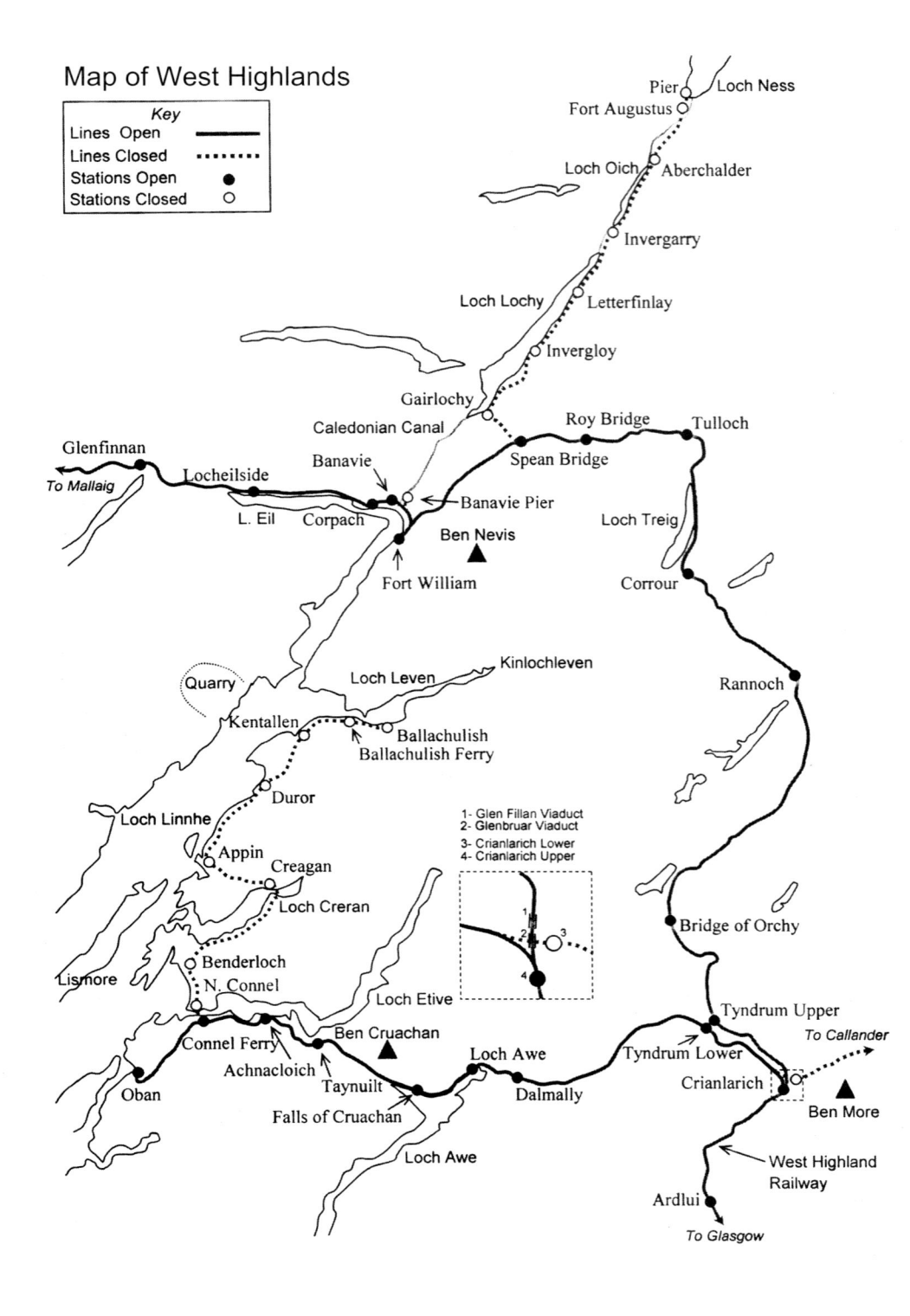

Key
- Lines Open ———
- Lines Closed - - - -
- Stations Open ●
- Stations Closed ○

Pier, Loch Ness, Fort Augustus, Loch Oich, Aberchalder, Invergarry, Loch Lochy, Letterfinlay, Invergloy, Gairlochy, Caledonian Canal, Roy Bridge, Tulloch, Spean Bridge, Glenfinnan, Locheilside, Banavie, L. Eil, Corpach, Banavie Pier, Ben Nevis, Loch Treig, Corrour, To Mallaig, Fort William, Kinlochleven, Loch Leven, Quarry, Kentallen, Ballachulish, Ballachulish Ferry, Rannoch, Loch Linnhe, Duror, Appin, Creagan, Loch Creran, Lismore, Benderloch, N. Connel, Loch Etive, Bridge of Orchy, Oban, Connel Ferry, Achnacloich, Ben Cruachan, Taynuilt, Falls of Cruachan, Loch Awe, Dalmally, Tyndrum Upper, Tyndrum Lower, Crianlarich, Ben More, To Callander, Loch Awe, West Highland Railway, Ardlui, To Glasgow

Inset:
1 - Glen Fillan Viaduct
2 - Glenbruar Viaduct
3 - Crianlarich Lower
4 - Crianlarich Upper

Chapter Two

Branches of the Callander and Oban Railway

The Lochearnhead, St Fillans and Comrie Railway:

'The Missing Link'

Developing a railway system can be akin to 'joining the dots'- a game at which railway promoters excelled in the nineteenth century. The fifteen mile gap between Comrie and Balquhidder joined two railway routes: the Callander and Oban Railway (C&OR) and the Crieff and Comrie Railway with its links to Perth and Central Scotland. Once linked, new routes could be opened up with the potential of generating new business. It was not always a good business model.

Backers considered that an extension westwards through the Upper Strathearn valley from Comrie, to link with the C&OR could be a popular route attracting tourists, particularly from the east coast. From the east, the railway had already reached Crieff in 1856 with a nine mile branch from the Scottish Central Railway (SCR) Stirling to Perth line, Glen Eagles Branch. A further route to Crieff, from Methven Junction (an extension of a short branch from Perth, itself a major railway centre), opened ten years later. The railway reached Comrie in 1893 and the dots were almost joined.

If the link to the Callander and Oban was completed then there was potential for tourists to extend their journey through grand Scottish scenery and reach as far west as Oban, with access to the islands, or even a circular route through Callander and back to the cities—a day out in style. Of course the natural beauty of the Upper Strathearn Valley could not be ignored—Loch Earn and its surrounding countryside would also encourage many tourists to stop and explore, who would have otherwise simply passed the end of Loch Earn heading for Crianlarich. Passenger traffic was thought likely to be significant, with the railway offering cheaper fares than coaches using the road and more comfort than those travelling by Shank's pony (on foot). Agricultural produce from the area could be delivered to new markets and sheep and cattle could avoid the exhausting journey along drove roads to the central belt. All it required was someone with vision to provide a lead and drive the project forward. Indeed, it was very a similar prospectus to that of the Callander and Oban and it was already in operation.

If the C&OR owed so much to the vision and persistence of John Anderson, then the same is true of the railways between Balquhidder Junction and Crieff. Colonel David Williamson, a local laird, supplied the energy and drive to overcome many obstacles to connect firstly Comrie to Crieff and then the extension west to link with the C&OR at Balquhidder Junction. Being one of the main landowners David Williamson felt duty bound to promote a railway to Comrie to help develop the economy of the Upper Strathearn Valley.

The bill authorising the railway was passed in 1865 but due to lack of funding both from local subscribers and the Caledonian Railway (CR) who were unable to provide any capital, partly because they were experiencing their own financial problems at the time, the construction of the line stalled for a quarter of a century. Despite valiant attempts to raise interest and none too subtle blackmail attempts to involve the CR, by threatening them with the North British Railway (NBR), it was 1890 before another parliamentary bill was obtained. With a strongly argued case Colonel Williamson was able to convince the Parliamentary Select Committee and overcame objections from other landowners. A railway into the Upper Strathearn Valley was also a step closer when the CR agreed to operate the new route. The following year the first turf was cut by his wife and by 1893 the six mile route was open between Crieff and Comrie. By 1898 with mounting financial problems caused by disappointing revenues and the continuing threat of litigation from the contractors who built the railway, the company was in trouble. A fairly generous offer from the CR meant that local investors did not lose out. The CR were now in a better financial position and the 'buy-out' made sense, given that they were already investing in the next railway along the Strathearn valley from Comrie to Lochearnhead.

The Lochearnhead, St Fillans and Comrie Railway (LSF&CR) completed the fifteen mile missing 'east-west' link between Comrie and the C&OR route. The railway was authorised in 1897 and was opened by 1905. This time there was no reluctance from the CR to provide finance and they invested half of the capital. With additional support from banks and brokers, the rest of the capital was soon raised. Colonel Williamson was still involved as a director, and probably because the route began on his Lednock estate near Comrie this time he was invited to cut the first turf in June 1899. The railway opened as far as St Fillans on 1st October 1901. It was built in two stages, firstly west from Comrie to St Fillans, at the eastern edge of Loch Earn, and then on to

Lochearnhead, along the north side of Loch Earn, where the railway had to turn south for two miles before it could join up with the C&OR, at Balquhidder. The railway was single track for its entire length, apart from passing loops. After the successful introduction of concrete on the Mallaig extension it was widely used as a building material for the viaducts, retaining walls and tunnel on the new line. There were several disputes over the siting of bridges which ensured that the railway did not spoil the environment. This was not so much altruistic than ensuring that the railway did not blight the view of the countryside for the local landowners! Surprisingly some of the disputes involved Colonel Williamson who now needed every penny from the builders to avoid bankruptcy. He was not alone, for by the time the section to St Fillans was almost complete the company had run out of money and an approach had to be made to the CR, who eventually took over the company within a year of the route opening as far as St Fillans. Landowners on this next section were even more difficult to deal with and the unexpected death of a local contractor led to many navvies being put out of work and starving. The locals did their best to support the navvies but many were forced to seek work elsewhere. Eventually the final section opened on 1st May 1905.

The hopes of traffic using the route to cross the country from the Highlands to Perth and Dundee with freight and livestock never materialised. The route did not generate sufficient revenue and traffic was light. Wartime economies closed Lochearnhead temporarily, during the First World War, and it was not until after the depression that there was an increase in passenger traffic. The route was used for excursions – Dundee to Oban, Crieff to Wemyss Bay on the Clyde Coast, and day trips from as far away as Aberdeen and Kilmarnock. A few excursions scheduled a stop at St Fillans. The Second World War stopped the excursion traffic and it never restarted, unless the extra traffic created by the delivery of prisoners of war to local camps is counted. Passenger traffic on the trains was hampered by relatively high fares compared to the buses. The route between Balquhidder Junction and Comrie was closed to passengers in 1951 as was the service between Crieff and Perth. The construction of a hydroelectric scheme near Glen Lednock kept the Balquhidder line open for freight until 1959. By 1953 the service from Comrie through Crieff using the Gleneagles (formerly Crieff Junction) branch with carriages for both Glasgow and Edinburgh was reduced to one train each way per day and the timings were not convenient for commuters. The railbus service, only introduced in 1958 to help reduce costs, ceased in 1964 by which time only two rail buses reached Comrie each day. The 'missing-link' had finally been broken.

Exploring the Railway Heritage

The route in this section is covered by the following maps: Explorer 365 and 368.

There were stations at Balquhidder Junction, Lochearnhead (2 miles from Balquhidder Junction), St Fillans (9.5 miles) and Comrie (15.25 miles).
The easiest sections to explore are between Balquhidder Junction and Lochearnhead, stopping where the cycle route links up with the old Callander and Oban line and from near Dalveich Farm (east of Lochearnhead, off the A85 (614244)) to St Fillans. St Fillans to Comrie involves several detours. The absence of a bus service between Comrie and Lochearnhead requires the use of a taxi (be sure to book beforehand) or cars being positioned at the end of sections.

The junction between the LSF&CR and the C&OR put the Comrie line at a disadvantage since traffic going on to Oban had to reverse. The junction also required considerable ground works to ensure that the two railways could exchange traffic with the Comrie line being at a lower level. The existing station complex, on the C&OR, originally known as Lochearnhead, was removed and shifted about 170 yards west and the ground level lowered. For several hundred yards the road had to be shifted north and the C&OR route also moved. With the road being at a lower height than the trackbed a subway had to be constructed, to allow access to the island platform, which at 800 foot long and 45 foot wide, was substantial. A second platform, on the A84 side of the station was also constructed and was used by northbound trains on the C&OR line. An engine shed, signal box (one of two at the station) and sidings filled the space where the two lines started to diverge.

Today the white glazed bricks of the subway and entrance stairway still draw attention from passing motorists. Indeed from the road

Balquhidder Station, entrance to underpass

the scene would be recognised by someone who knew the station when it opened. The Post Office opposite is now a restaurant and the station façade is all that remains for the platform and other buildings have been removed and replaced with the Balquhidder Braes Caravan Park (574210). The C&OR route once crossed

Balquhidder Station entrance stairway

over the road just north of the station site with the two lines diverging before drawing closer together, although at very different heights, on the steep valley side near Lochearnhead. On leaving the station the Comrie route kept to the south side of the road, crossing moorland at a falling gradient of one in sixty. The journey is now through woodland but the trackbed is still clear.

One mile on, the railway eventually crossed over the road and approached the Edinchip or Kendrum Viaduct. Road realignment and removal of the road bridge has altered this section but the viaduct now marks the first part of the Comrie Railway to be used as a cycle path (583224). The fifty-six foot high concrete viaduct has seven arches of forty feet and a central metal girder span of eighty feet over the Kendrum Burn. There are five arches to the south of the girder span and two to the north. The central portion was removed for scrap after closure but has been replaced by a narrower span when it was reopened as a cycle path. Some locals refer to the new span as the 'Sydney bridge replica' due to its appearance. The funds for reconstruction were raised in part in memory of Nigel Hester, a musician, killed while cycling on the A9.

The cycle path continues through woodland until the southern edge of Loch Earn, where the cycle path climbs the hillside to reach the C&OR route. The Comrie Railway continues towards Lochearnhead. The conditions underfoot can be poor as the trackbed approaches the station passing under several overbridges. It is easier to bypass this section and use the A84 to reach the north of the station site, next to the Lochearnhead Viaduct.

The station site (587238) is well preserved, thanks to the Hertfordshire Scouts who use it as a base for outdoor activities. The site is often busy, and while the scouts are very welcoming, permission should be sought before

Lochearnhead Station site

exploring the site. The nearly 200-yard island platform and station buildings remain as does the entrance to the passenger subway. The style is similar to Balquhidder. On the southern approach was a signal box, now removed. A loading bay and goods shed was to the north-west of the station. Trees now fringe the site blocking the once magnificent views eastwards along Loch Earn and north towards Glenogle.

From Lochearnhead Station the line curved east crossing over the A84, by a rail bridge now removed, to reach the nine-arched Lochearnhead (Glenogle) Viaduct. The nine arches each with a forty-foot span, cross the Ogle Burn to reach the hillside to the north of Loch Earn - a majestic sweep and an impressive bridging of a major obstacle. The viaduct can still be accessed although the eastern edge is now blocked by a house. With trees restricting views, probably the best view is from the trackbed of the C&OR high on the hillside above.

From the viaduct the trackbed snaked along the loch side, 100 feet above it on the slopes of Achraw Hill, slowly losing height. Between the trackbed and the loch is the road. Looking south, across the loch, are the majestic peaks of Stuc a Chroin and Ben Vorlich. The first mile and a half is quite difficult but at Dalveich Farm at the mouth of the valley of Glen Beich the trackbed, on an embankment at this point, can be accessed from the road and the trackbed followed until St Fillans with only minor detours. Conditions underfoot can be difficult, however, as timber extraction churns up the land.

Eastwards from Dalveich Farm there is a steadily rising gradient with only minor dips until St Fillans. Coupled with extensive planting of conifers, the effect is to divorce the walker from the rumble of the traffic along the

Loch Earn from Oban train. Crieff branch train on Lochearnhead Viaduct 1951

sometimes busy A85 which hugs the shoreline of the loch. The elevated view produces a different impression of the glens etched into the side of the hills on the south side of the loch, leading to the summits of Stuc a Chroin and Ben Vorlich (both known as Munros as they are over 3000 feet high). Stuc a Chroin lies to the south-west of Ben Vorlich, closer to Strathyre. The hills towering above the trackbed to the north of the loch are also impressive.

The many streams that tumble down the hillside created extra work for the railway engineers but their efforts have largely survived the demise of the railway. A three span concrete viaduct was required to cross Allt na-h-Atha near the farmhouse of Derry and remains intact. A break in the woodlands, shortly after the viaduct, allows for panoramic views over the loch and valley and the busy activity on the loch, well-known for a variety of water sports.

Timber extraction has removed the trackbed in places but the direction is clear. In a gap between the planted woods the railway reached Glentarken. The narrow and deep gorge that the Glentarken has gouged out of the hillside was a difficult obstacle to overcome. Sadly the single span metal girder bridge has been dismantled and only the concrete abutments remain. A steep and tricky detour to the loch side is required with a steep scramble required on the far side to regain the trackbed. On the approach to the eastern abutment is one of only two access bridges over the railway in this section.

Through Glentarken Wood the trackbed continues crossing over Allt an Fhionn by a five arch viaduct. Construction costs were high on the approach to St Fillans with streams again having to be crossed. An access road twists under the disused railway requiring a concrete retaining wall and arches on the outskirts of St Fillans. A deep waterlogged cutting then leads to a short sixty-

Abutments of Glentarken Viaduct near St. Fillans

two yard tunnel. Concrete faced and lined, the tunnel has been fenced off requiring a further scramble to reach the other side. The tunnel was a late addition to the construction plans, but was added so as not to devalue the local villas, by concealing the railway. Houses have been built on the embankment of the railway trackbed as it approaches St Fillans Station. A final missing rail bridge leads to the long concrete faced embankment on the approach to the station. Now a caravan site, the station (700244) has been well preserved. Indeed so well preserved that Historic Scotland has prevented the owner from making changes which alter its character. This seems slightly unfair since the owner had developed the site, while maintaining the railway links, and the restrictions imposed make the site more difficult to sell.

A long driveway leads to the station building. The prominent brick face chimney, the steeply graded roof and the wooden lattice effect sides would be instantly recognisable to those who travelled by rail. The canopy has been renewed but the wrought iron supports remain. The windows in the side supports of the canopy, which would have offered some protection from the wind, have been covered up. The concrete platforms have been retained but between them there is now a children's play park, not waiting trains. Further along the platform, almost lost amongst caravans,

St. Fillans tunnel

St. Fillans Station

is the original brick-based signal box, with a hipped roof and slight overhang. Maybe Historic Scotland have a point - this is a well preserved example of a late Victorian railway site but replacing even roof tiles on a like-for-like basis is a costly burden to impose on an individual. The station is to the rear of the village at the end of the inevitable Station Road.

Within two days of the station opening, the engine shunting wagons for a goods train was derailed in the goods yard but this was not typical of the line's safety record, which was very good. The village at the eastern end of Loch Earn is named after an early Celtic missionary. The saint was believed to have lived on St Fillans Hill, a distinctive small hill, which lies to the south of the former railway and the A85, on the eastern edge of the golf course.

St. Fillans Station site today

Beyond the station site the trackbed steadily loses height as it gradually draws closer to the A85. To the left of the trackbed is a rocky outcrop, painted to resemble a crocodile. With its bright colours, once maintained by the CR, it is still a landmark situated to the north of the railway fence. Formerly it was known as the 'Pig Rock'—so much for evolution.

The trackbed then passed under the A85 and almost immediately crossed the River Earn by the Tynrioch bowstring bridge. The next section starts through open countryside but then enters Dundurn Wood as the trackbed again draws close to the River Earn. The railway engineers had to blast their way through a ridge of solid rock. The moss covered rock faces of the cuttings now look abandoned—the place that time forgot. The River Earn is again crossed, this time by the three-arched Dundurn Viaduct before the Dalchonzie Halt is reached on the east side of what was once a level crossing. A signal box controlled the level crossing and access to a siding. The platform and a basic wooden shelter were opposite the signal box. The signal box has been converted into a house. Wooden steps once extended from the door at the side of the house to ground level, beside the track. The level crossing gates remain only on the St Fillans side. Passengers alighting at Dalchonzie Halt, opened in 1903, had to inform the guard at the previous station. Just east of the level crossing there was a tragic accident, in August 1904, when a mother having crossed the line to reach a baker's van, parked on the A85, noticed that her young daughter of twenty months had wandered onto the line. Racing back to collect her both she and her daughter were killed by a train.

The trackbed then runs close to the A85 as it turns south-east on the approach to Comrie. A quicker and simpler route to follow would be to

Dalchonzie looking to Perth

turn right at the site of the level crossing and follow the minor road until the abutments of the Tullybannocher Viaduct are reached. This avoids a detour caused by the missing sections of the viaduct.

Near Tullybannocher, on the western approach to Comrie (close to the Drummond Trout Farm and Fishery) the trackbed is lost and the metal girder sections of the Tullybannocher Viaduct over the River Earn and a minor road have been removed. The concrete abutments remain. The trackbed then continues alongside the Sawdust Path, associated with the bobbins made here for the local thread industry. The trackbed then crossed 'The Ross' by a minor road, but the rail bridge is missing. Beside the road closer to Comrie is 'Earthquake House'. Comrie, sitting on the Highland Boundary Fault, is nicknamed the 'Shaky Toun' because of the minor earth tremors it has long experienced. The world's first seismometer was set up here in 1840. The 'Earthquake House' was set up in 1869, and the interior can be viewed through the windows.

The trackbed swings north-east to cross the River Earn for the fourth and final time. Two arches of the viaduct remain to the south but the rest have been removed. Eleven masonry arches were required to cross both the River Earn and Dundas Street on the other side of the river. Two girder sections spanned the river and street. Slightly to the west of the viaduct the Water of Ruchill joins the River Earn from the south. Situated between the Water of Ruchill and the B827 was Cultybraggan Camp, a former Prisoner-of-War camp for captured Afrika Korp and eventually hard line Nazis. The camp was later converted to become the centre for the Scottish Government in event of another World War but is no longer kept for this purpose. Another POW camp was set up at nearby Dalginross and was used to intern Italian and low risk Germans. Prisoners arrived by train, after a long journey, usually from Channel Ports.

On the north side of the River Earn the line of the railway can be traced along School Road, across Nurse's Lane (formerly Mill Road), eventually crossing the River Lednock, flowing south to join up with the River Earn. The name Comrie means the 'meeting of the waters' and it is an appropriate name. The railway bridge is missing with only the abutments remaining, but has been replaced by a wooden walkway. The route then passed under the A85, again, before reaching the station site which is now occupied by a caravan park.

It was here that the Crieff and Comrie and the LSF&CR met. Before the opening of the railway west of Comrie the railway stopped next to the road. There was a signal box on the approach which controlled access to the sidings south of the station. A wooden station building was constructed with a short canopy. When the railway to Balquhidder was opened, another platform with a similar, but not identical, wooden building, was built to the north of the line with a connecting footbridge. The LSF&CR was not the success hoped for but did open up this beautiful valley and made it more accessible to many more people. Colonel David Williamson should be proud of his efforts to bring prosperity to the area.

The Killin Railway

'Watching the pennies'

The story of the Killin Railway (KR) is one of survival against the odds for thirty-seven years. Like the trains, struggling to climb the continuous gradient of one in fifty from Killin to the junction with the C&OR, it was an uphill struggle for this small rural line to survive. Revenues were meagre and margins were eye-wateringly tight. When the nameboard for 'Killin Junction' station arrived without the 'Killin' – the company waited until the original Killin Station, on the C&OR, was renamed Glenoglehead and the two names could be paired up. Maybe that approach reflected contemporary values, where everything was individually produced and valued, but it was certainly watching the pennies. The Bank of Scotland provided free premises for forty years which helped, but even basic maintenance such as a fresh coat of paint for Killin Station had to be debated and as a result the station would never have won any 'best kept station' awards.

Killin Junction looking east 1956

Financial arrangements with the CR, who worked the route, had to be constantly renegotiated otherwise the secretary, A.R. Robertson, would not have received any salary or indeed would any loan repayments have been made. The secretary of the KR even had to ask the CR for a free train pass to Glasgow to argue his case for extra money. John Anderson, who knew the value of money through his efforts to develop the C&OR, had many dealings with Robertson, whose background was in banking. His dealings with Anderson displayed a sometimes naive understanding of railway procedures and operations. Robertson required much support and advice with issues as basic as signalling requirements and even the number of tickets to order.

The railway had its beginnings with the Marquis of Breadalbane, who had a reputation for proposing railway schemes, such as the Scottish Grand Junction Railway, and who lived at his ancestral home of Taymouth Castle to the east of Loch Tay. He thought that the steamer service on Loch Tay could be augmented by a railway delivering to the western shore, both cargos and people. Rebuffed both by the C&OR and its owners the CR, the Marquis went it alone by holding a meeting, under his chairmanship in August 1882, to propose a railway for Killin. The Marquis contributed generously. John Anderson, however, bought some shares on behalf of the C&OR but showed little enthusiasm for the new branch whose prospects he obviously didn't rate.

The proposals, however, caught the imagination of the locals. From farmers to tradesmen and probably the owners of illicit stills, all came forward to contribute. No one objected, so no Act of Parliament was required, only a Board of Trade Certificate. Within a year work began but the first contractor, who had hopelessly underestimated costs, went bankrupt due to the costs of the viaduct over the River Dochart being higher than estimated. The construction was continued with another contractor and the railway opened on 13 March 1886 for freight and on 1 April the same year for passengers. The line survived as an independent, operated by the CR, until the regrouping of 1923, when it became part of the LMS grouping.

The new railway was an improvement for the people of Killin. The C&OR having kept to the high ground as the railway turned west from Glen Ogle into Glen Dochart, had provided Killin with a station named after the village but not close enough to be of much practical use with the distance between the two being three and a half miles and a climb of 550 feet. The new railway brought the train right into the village itself and through to the shores of Loch Tay. The five and a quarter mile railway travelled through breathtaking scenery from the grandeur of Glen Dochart to the shoreline of Loch Tay with views including the highest peak in Perthshire, Ben Lawers. The lure for tourists included Killin, itself a most attractive village at the western end of Loch

Tay found between the rivers Dochart and Lochay, both of which feed into the loch. The magnificent Falls of Dochart, located within the village were worth visiting at any time of year and the option of a fourteen and a half mile cruise to Kenmore at the eastern end of Loch Tay made Killin an attractive destination for tourists. Tourism was the most important revenue earner and on some summer days, more than one train operated on the line at one time, which was against Board of Trade regulations.

Other attempts to increase business were not successful. Farmers were persuaded to try the railway to take their sheep to market in Perth. Using the KR meant a long detour, down Glen Ogle, east to Comrie and then through Crieff to reach Perth - a distance of 51 miles. With poor facilities, no shelter for sheep or easy loading, the farmers soon opted for the shorter route east to Aberfeldy at the other end of Loch Tay and then Perth.

For the journey to Loch Tay from Killin Junction the CR supplied two locomotives, known locally as 'Killin Pugs'. Six trains a day made the climb to connect with the C&OR at Killin Junction with many of the trains mixed – goods and passengers. The passenger service from the section between Killin and Loch Tay ceased at the start of the Second World War and the rest of the line closed in September 1965 after the Glen Ogle landslide.

The railway did gain notoriety in the 1935 film *The 39 Steps* where the hero Richard Hannay discovers a map showing the Killin Railway and surroundings with a fictitious local estate to the north circled in ink. This probably represented the greatest national exposure for the KR! Hannay leaves London for the estate, by train, and is forced to leave the train on the Forth rail bridge with police searching the passenger compartments for him. Next day, by foot, he arrives at the house – an amazing journey in twenty-four hours! The train would have struggled to keep up with him! Incidentally in the 1959 remake of *The 39 Steps* the hero is seen cycling through Killin (called Glenkirk in the film) past the Falls of Dochart.

Exploring the Railway Heritage

The route in this section is covered by the following maps:
Explorer; 365, 378

There were stations at Killin (4 miles from Killin Junction) and Loch Tay (5.25 miles). There are three routes to the site of Killin Junction where the exploration begins; after all it's easier to walk downhill and you can't leave your car close to Killin Junction. The first option is to walk up the disused railway from the A85, near the junction (Lix Toll) with the A827 and retrace your steps. It is also possible to walk from the site of Glenoglehead Station on the Callander and Oban route and reach the start of the KR at Killin Junction. A bus from Callander provides a limited service and can drop you at Glenoglehead.

Ledcharrie Burn to Killin

The third option is to catch a bus from Killin (service very limited) in the direction of Crianlarich and be dropped off at Ledcharrie Farm (506282) on the A85 to follow the first part of the seven mile public path that leads over the hills to Balquhidder Glen. The former C&OR railway track is reached at the Glen Dochart Viaduct (508274) over the Ledcharrie Burn where you turn east. A short and interesting excursion west to reach the site of the Luib Viaduct before retracing your steps does not add much to the length of the journey and is described in the chapter on the Callander and Oban route.

The three-arched Glen Dochart Viaduct is braced with old rails and has been repaired with bricks. The middle arch crosses the burn. East of the Glen Dochart Viaduct the trackbed, high on the hillside, provides a platform to view the countryside. To the west is the mighty Ben More. To the north are endless hills and as you progress east further peaks are glimpsed on the horizon. Further up the rock strewn hillside from the trackbed are more peaks which separate Glen Dochart from the Braes of Balquhidder. Towards the east the view is increasingly blocked by the approaching woodlands. Down in the valley, on the far side of the A85, the River Dochart meanders towards the unseen Loch Tay with farms scattered on the hillsides.

The trackbed is in good condition and still lined for stretches with the original fencing. A stone overbridge allowed access to the hillside for farmers and probably shooting parties. As the woodland that surrounds Killin Junction approaches, Ardchyle Viaduct, which towers above the burn from which it's named, is crossed and marks the change from barren hillside to forest. The three round-headed arches are skewed and the viaduct shows some signs of deterioration.

The approach to Killin Junction (530297) through woodlands is well preserved with the trackbed being used as an access road. The former junction site is found in a clearing. The concrete edge of the exchange island platform remains but the platform is in a poor state, and the single platform to the south which served the c&or has been removed. In the foliage the base of a signal post remains and to the north among the trees ruined cottages which served the railwaymen. The footbridge has gone along with the buildings on the island platform. The brick base of one of the two signal boxes remains. The station was 300 feet above the nearby A85 but there was no road access. Neither (and this is more surprising) was there access for locals wishing to travel by train. The 'station' was an exchange platform and the kr would not permit access for the inhabitants of Glen Dochart despite their complaints. Only those arriving by train were permitted to use the station. How those who journeyed by train must have enjoyed the views before the trees were planted. The station perched high on a hillside, and once surrounded by only a few pine trees must have been a very remote and special place.

The kr lost height quickly as it left the junction site and was soon well below the height of the c&or which is quickly lost to view. The trackbed runs parallel to the A85 for the first mile, and crosses over an old military road on its descent. New access roads have been made by the forestry. Surprisingly, a few remnants of the railway remain, such as telegraph poles with vee-shaped metal tops. There are cottages to the south at Wester Lix, as the A85 which by now has turned sharply south to enter Glen Ogle is approached, but the bridge over the A85, near Lix Toll where the A827 joins it, is missing. Ben Lawers can be clearly seen ahead, a view that those who travelled by train would have enjoyed earlier.

The continuation of the route on the far side leads into Achmore Woods. The views are lost to be replaced by the silence of the woods. The National Cycle Route No.7 joins the trackbed from Glenoglehead. From here the trackbed is well-maintained and a pleasant walk with concrete drainage channels for much

Killin Junction

The 1.42 pm to Killin Junction at Killin 1961

of its length and a collection of concrete sleepers that no one has removed. Overhead power cables cross the trackbed just before a stream and a most unusual double decker bridge. The lower part is a culvert, allowing a stream to flow under the trackbed but on top is a sheep creep with a concrete tunnel again under the trackbed.

As the village of Killin approaches, the River Dochart, the road and trackbed, all draw closer together. The gradient, still dropping in height, enters a cutting crossed by a metal span overbridge before the trackbed stops abruptly where the cycle route turns left. This is the first real obstacle. A detour by the Falls of Dochart to the station site is advised. The trackbed can be traced but with house building it will become increasingly difficult. The Falls of Dochart demand attention and usually there are people photographing the water cascading over the rocks or when the water is lower, scrambling over rocks to sit and contemplate the views. When the railway was open it was a popular walk from the station to the Falls. To the north the hills dominate Killin and to the south are woods with more hills on the horizon. As the water tumbles under the road bridge it swirls round the little island of Inchbuie, the burial ground of the Clan MacNab.

A walk down the main street gives plenty of opportunity for refreshment before following the signs for the car park beside the road depot. After all the scenery encountered, the station site is a let down with no trace remaining. The simple wooden station building facing Loch Tay, with a roof sloping to the rear with a very short overhanging canopy beside a single platform, has long gone. The platform was short and 'specials' often had to stop in stages to allow passengers to disembark. The station was described as dirty, not surprisingly, because the railway company received payment from the local council to dump rubbish at it. They were, however, encouraged to dump the rubbish in such a way as to prepare for the construction of a second set of rails which of course were never needed.

The trackbed is still intact and in use as a walk way. By walking back in the direction of Killin Junction the Dochart Viaduct can be crossed. The viaduct is the second oldest example of a plain concrete railway structure in Britain. Its five concrete arches are supported by badly stained stone piers. The arches at each end are skewed. The castellated parapet is in poor condition and a wire fence has been built for safety along each side. The view towards Ben Lawers is very clear above the tree lined river. To the north the trackbed continues as a walk way, until the site of Loch Tay Station. This is the flat section of the KR along the western shore of Loch Tay. The River Lochay is crossed by a three span flat metal girder bridge, supported on concrete pillars. Originally the piers were of wood but these were split during their first winter, by blocks of ice.

The tree lined route continues beside a wooded hillside past the ruin of Finlarig Castle, the seat of the Campbells of Finlarig. The ruin is on the far side of Pier Road where the road starts to run parallel to the trackbed. The railway ended at an engine shed. Just before the shed was Loch Tay Station (583345) which consisted of a single platform and a basic station building in the same style as Killin but facing west. The station building is in the private grounds of a house but can be glimpsed from the end of Pier Road. A siding led to the pier where steamers once departed to cross to Kenmore at the other end of the loch. The site of a crannog, one of many around Loch

Loch Tay Station site

Tay, is found on an islet just to the east of the station site and a walk back by the shores of Loch Tay to the railway bridge and then Killin station site, is a pleasant option.

This section closed in 1939 but continued to be used by the engines travelling to their shed. Work on a nearby hydroelectric scheme saw the section in use again around 1950. Finlarig Power Station, a hydroelectric scheme, is beyond the station site but not visible from Pier Road.

Life was never anything less than a struggle for those who ran the KR, which seems unfair when it enabled visitors to enjoy the grandeur of this picturesque and remote part of Scotland. Those who ran the company had to make every penny count, so the fact that the railway survived for as long as it did suggests that they had some success.

The Ballachulish Branch

'Anderson's Gamble'

Maybe John Anderson was becoming over confident, since battling his way to Oban against the odds because he now joined the fight for a line to Inverness. With Inverness already seen as an attractive destination, the West Highland Railway (WHR), having reached Fort William in 1894, was interested in developing a route through the Great Glen to the capital of the Highlands. The Highland Railway (HR) looked on this proposed intrusion with alarm. It was not the first, although other proposals had not got beyond being plans on paper. There was now to be a railway at the other end of the Great Glen. The HR were very protective of what they saw as their interests, and considered building a route to Fort William to counter the WHR plans. In the midst of this posturing, in October 1894, John Anderson declared his intention to build a branch from the C&OR, round the Appin peninsula to Ballachulish, north along the shores of Loch Linnhe to Fort William and then through the Great Glen to Inverness, without the help of other railway companies. It was a bold initiative.

The opposition to John Anderson's plans was extremely strong. The HR and the WHR backers, the NBR, agreed to delay any developments in the Great Glen for ten years. The CR, whom Anderson had tried to exclude from his plans, backed a WHR scheme to build a branch from Fort William south to Ballachulish, basically the same route as the C&OR wished to take. With both the NBR and the CR lined up against him and with an extension into the Great Glen also likely to incur the wrath of the HR the odds were stacked against Anderson. Showing his usual tenacity, however, he started negotiations for a railway station to be built on a former prison site in Fort William and surveyed a route as far as Banavie, near Fort William, where his limited funds ran out. Despite last minute efforts to persuade backers, John Anderson had to abandon his parliamentary bill, less than four months later. His bold gamble had failed.

Out of all this activity, however there remained the suggestion that Ballachulish still deserved a railway connection, but as a branch line and not part of a through route. Both the C&OR and the WHR showed interest in the world renowned slate quarries at Ballachulish. The WHR proposals, however, encountered more opposition. The people of Fort William resented the railway for building on the foreshore and 'spoiling the town' and did not wish the railway extended south, building on more of the shore front. The quarry owners at Ballachulish were also not keen on a rail bridge over Loch Leven, which might interfere with shipments from the quarries, despite a central swinging section incorporated in the design.

Anderson's proposals started at Connel Ferry Station, on their existing route to Oban, and required the bridging of two sea lochs, Loch Etive and Loch Creran; such is the indented nature of the coastline. The route cut also across the Benderloch peninsula and wound around the Appin coastline to reach Ballachulish. There were changes to the original route and the siting of the stations. Originally Loch Creran was going to be bridged further west near Port Appin and a hotel was planned for this site. The hotel was built but never opened and became a private house. The crossing was eventually made further east.

Argyll Council wanted the proposed rail bridges to carry road vehicles also but this was eventually rejected as the C&OR wanted to work this route independently. With no road through Glen Coe and with no road crossings of these lochs, travelling in the area was difficult with poor roads and, without bridges, requiring long detours. This issue caused much local debate, for many years, and a lot of unnecessary friction. The John Anderson of old would surely have been more sensitive to the loss of local goodwill and encouraged local involvement, but a virtual monopoly on transport in the Appin peninsula proved more important to railway revenues.

Both companies submitted bills to parliament and both acts were passed on the same day, 7th August 1896 but the WHR was denied permission to bridge Loch Leven and abandoned their plans. However, given that the slate quarries were in decline and that the opening of the aluminium works at Kinlochleven were a few years away then the squabble over who would provide a railway for Ballachulish does seem more like empire building and not good economic planning.

The twenty-eight mile Ballachulish branch opened in August 1903 and was one of the last branch lines opened in Britain. It serviced remote communities and the Ballachulish slate works and after its construction the aluminium smelting works at the eastern end of Loch Leven. Up to twenty container wagons daily took bauxite to the aluminium works from the terminus of the railway at Ballachulish. With the slate quarries already in decline and a small local population, the railway, while very popular with locals travelling to Oban, especially the sometimes exuberant last train from Oban on a Saturday evening, had to struggle to survive. With the aluminium ore shipments removed from the branch to the West Highland line in 1965, the route survived only a further year.

However, a renaissance of sorts has happened. The outstanding natural beauty of the land has encouraged SUSTRANS to convert as much of the route as possible into a cycle track, which will end ironically at Inverness, a hundred years too late. The remnants of the line, especially the magnificent cantilever bridge crossing Loch Leven at the dramatic Falls of Lora, and the now converted rail bridge over Loch Creran, can still be appreciated and enjoyed.

Connel Ferry Bridge 1952

Exploring the Railway Heritage

The route in this section is covered by the following maps:
Explorer 376, 384

There were stations at North Connel (0.75 miles from Connel Ferry Station), Benderloch (3 miles), Creagan (10 miles), Appin (13.25 miles), Duror (19 miles), Kentallen (22.75 miles), Ballachulish Ferry (25.75 miles) and Ballachulish (27.75 miles).

Connel Ferry Bridge looking north 1938

The state of the railway trackbed has improved greatly over the last few years and as work continues to develop a cycle path, part of Sustrans Route 78, the condition of the route should further improve.

Trains travelling on the C&OR get a very impressive view of the principal feature on the Ballachulish Branch – the Connel Ferry Bridge. Located where Loch Etive narrowed to 690 feet, at the Falls of Lora, the cantilever bridge is the second longest in the United Kingdom (after the Forth Rail Bridge). The nature of its construction was determined by the Falls of Lora as the water from the loch at this point falls four feet. The ebb and flow of

Connel Ferry bridge

the tides here churns up the water which meant that it was not possible to construct a central pier. Construction of the bridge started on each shore with three thirty-eight and a half-foot masonry arches. Two main piers were then constructed with the cantilever spans resting on them. Anchored deep in the piers the steelwork edged out and up. The central span was 500 feet with the total length being 1044 feet. The bridge was fifty-four feet high. A footway was constructed beside the railway. The locals tried for years to be allowed to cross the bridge and for a road to be constructed. Much to the annoyance of the locals the C&OR refused. John Anderson wanted a pay back and the council would not negotiate. It was travel by train or not at all! In 1909 the railway did introduce a motor charabanc which allowed cars to be loaded on it and cross the bridge for a payment. The motor charabanc had to reverse as there was no provision for turning it.

Only when permission was granted for a chain ferry crossing Loch Etive in 1913 did the C&OR change their minds and suddenly decide to build a roadway for vehicles. The footpath was adapted and arrangements made so that trains and cars could use the bridge but not at the same time. Toll charges proved unpopular, but the railway company claimed that they were only trying to get a return on an expensive investment.

Today the bridge, with traffic lights in operation as the deck is narrow, allows traffic to flow in one direction at a time. A road leads up to the bridge from the

A85. As the road climbs towards the bridge a minor road branches. The minor road is quickly crossed by two bridges. The second carries the railway to Oban. The first was also intended as a rail bridge if a triangular junction had been completed, allowing trains from Oban to run directly onto the line. The single arch bridge with wing walls, like most bridges on the branch is constructed of concrete. A casting gives the impression of a segmental arch but the railway was constructed when concrete was becoming the main material for construction and dressed stone was a more expensive alternative. The trackbed to each side of the single arch bridge however, has not been completed.

As the approach road turns towards the bridge and the traffic lights, the original route of the railway from Connel Ferry Station can be traced leading through a deep rock-faced cutting to join up with the main line. The views from the bridge are panoramic and the swirling waters underneath, depending on the tide, are fascinating to watch. Across Connel Ferry Bridge, road realignment has removed any traces of North Connel Station (911348). Opened about six months after the railway started operating, it consisted of a wooden platform to the east of the line. The realigned road also bypasses the small community of North Connel. On the north side of Connel Ferry Bridge, Donald Sutherland playing an escaping German spy, abandoned his motorbike in the 1981 film *Eye of the Needle*. The bridge forms a dramatic backdrop to the scene.

The trackbed can be picked up near the entrance to Connel Airfield and as it approaches the Benderloch Caravan Park at North Ledaig it passes through a cutting crossed by several overbridges. The views over Ardmucknish Bay towards Lismore and further west to the Island of Mull are spectacular and must have provided a wonderful backdrop for travellers. Near Benderloch the widening of the road and the provision of a lay-by has removed the trackbed, which is lost until the station site. To the right are towering tree-topped cliff faces. There was little space for both road and railway at this point.

The station site in Benderloch (904381) was sited opposite the garage and Benderloch stores. The trackbed has been tarmacked and forms part of a safe walking route towards Lochnell Primary School at the north end of the village. This has removed most traces of the station leaving only a short section of concrete platform on each side of the track. There was a straight section of siding on a rising gradient in the area now occupied by a care home. There were also short sidings behind each platform. At the station there was a wooden signal box and the main buildings which were double-storey with a canopy over the platform with glass screens at each end. On the other side was a simpler waiting room with a canopy overhang. The platforms were to either side of a crossing loop, a common arrangement on this branch. The village of Benderloch is also known as Ledaig. The railway cut across the Benderloch peninsula; one of the few times it left the coastline. Beyond Benderloch the trackbed twists and turns beside the road (A828), with part of the trackbed being used by the sand and gravel quarry north of Benderloch.

Further on, the trackbed is disrupted by the entrance to the Sea Life Centre near Barcaldine, a popular tourist attraction, which operates an aquarium and seal rescue centre. The trackbed also parts from the company of the road near Barcaldine where the road turns slightly inland. A section of tree-lined cutting leads to a yacht store and then a pier used, amongst other things, to load quarry products onto boats. There was a halt at Barcaldine (964423), opened in 1913, located where the yachts are now stored, but all signs have been removed. It consisted of a single platform to the east of the line. The platform had a simple wooden shelter, with a cattle pen on the platform. There was also a siding to the south which ran behind the platform. Beyond the pier the railway crossed over a river, this time by a metal girder bridge. Surprisingly there are several tall trees growing from the decking. Shortly afterwards there was a rail bridge over the road which has been completely removed. A short section of cutting on the far side indicates where the railway then continued towards Creagan Bridge on an embankment, until close to the viaduct where it passed through a cutting, which was infilled when the road bridge was built. This section is now surrounded by trees but there are many views of Loch Creran. Creagan Station can also be seen across the loch.

The Creagan Bridge, sometimes known as the Creran Viaduct, consisted of two lattice girder spans of 150 feet placed on a central pier, forty feet

Barcaldine Halt 1950

Creagan Bridge 1950

above the high tide mark of the tidal loch. There was a single castellated granite approach span on each side. The approach spans were demolished in 1999 and the height of the piers reduced by six feet. The south pier was removed and replaced although the new pier used the old granite facing. The 'Mersey Mammoth' floating crane was required to lift the lattice girder spans off. Approach roads were constructed removing the trackbed immediately north and south of the bridge.

High above the roundabout north of the loch the trackbed resumes. The rail bridge over the road has been lost. The trackbed enters a tree lined cutting blasted through an outcrop of rock. The trackbed continues across a section of embankment, which crosses the road to Creagan Farm before reaching the station.

Creagan Station (970449) has been well preserved as a feature of Appin Holiday Homes, a caravan and chalet park. Its island platform, the only example on the branch, is complete with the single storey station building. Originally there was a signal box on the platform. The hip-roofed building with twin chimneys is complete with notice boards and even signage, although the signage is not original. The park owners see the station as an attractive feature. Beyond the building is the entrance to a pedestrian subway. The metal frame for the water tank is intact. With the backdrop of high hills and with its commanding views over the loch towards the Benderloch Mountains the railway must have been a most attractive place to wait for a train. One of the platforms was taken out of use in April 1927 and there was a siding to the east.

Between Creagan Station and Appin Station the trackbed is almost intact, although where the drainage has deteriorated, the ground can be muddy. The

Creagan Station looking south

trackbed initially climbs away from Creagan Station through low cuttings before crossing a two-arch concrete rail bridge over a burn. Nearer Appin the trackbed passes through fields before reaching the road. In Appin village a single track winds down to Port Appin, the ferry terminus for nearby Lismore Island. With hotels famous for their cuisine and the wonderful scenic views, the village is worth visiting. Appin Station (924473) was about a mile beyond the village at Portnacroish. The trackbed carried on a low embankment, ran beside Loch Laich, another sea loch. The railway, however, did not have to cross the loch but the inhabitants of Portnacroish did to reach the Free Church, near Port Appin.

A wooden bridge, built to celebrate the diamond jubilee of Queen Victoria in 1898, was very convenient for intending passengers of the railway, when the railway opened a few years later. Its structure has seen better days and is unique in Argyll as it crosses a salt marsh. Part of the trackbed has been tarmacked, as part of the 'walk to school' scheme. Ahead are the first views of Castle Stalker, a tower house built on an islet in the sea loch. It was built by Duncan Stewart in the fifteenth century and lay in ruins for two hundred years before restoration work began in 1965. For many it must provide one of the classic Scottish views – a castle on an island surrounded by grand views. For those walking the railway trackbed, the views are diminished by the local road depot. Castle Stalker was used, renamed as Castle Aargh at the end of the Monty Python film: *Monty Python and the Holy Grail.*

The curved concrete platforms of Appin Station remain intact and nearby the station cottages have unusual extensions. The railway then turned sharply north remaining at sea level as it passed several farms. The road also bends north but climbs steeply and drops to the level of the railway about a mile further on. Off the coast is Shuna Island, an uninhabited island with the remains of the sixteenth century Shuna Castle. Visible on the west side of Loch Linnhe, on the Morven peninsula, is Glensanda Quarry, which opened in 1986, and is one of the largest quarries in the world, producing over six million tonnes of granite a year and capable of producing fifteen million tonnes at capacity. Crushed granite, quarried 520 metres above sea level is dropped down a vertical shaft known as a 'glory hole' and then carried by conveyor belt to the coast to be transported. The set-up reduces the environmental impact of the operation.

North of Shuna Island the railway emerges beside Loch Linnhe. The views across the loch towards the eastern edge of the Ardgour peninsula are truly outstanding. Road widening means that the railway trackbed has been removed for long stretches between where the railway and road come together again. The boundary of Argyll Council and Highland Council lies opposite the tiny island of Eilean Balnagowan. The trackbed continues to cling to the coastline and after passing the remains of a ruined chapel near Keil, the next station at Duror (976542) is reached. Slightly to the south of the village, the station similar in construction to Benderloch Station, with a two storey building to the east of the line is now an attractive converted house with open views across Loch Linnhe. The platforms are still intact but the siding to the north east of the station has been landscaped.

North of Duror Station the trackbed and road veer inland and the railway crossed over the road to head further inland. The rail bridge has been removed. The village of Duror is situated in a narrow valley flanked to the east by steep sloped hills. The trackbed now assumes the air of a country railway cutting through fields. The trackbed is used for access for cottages and forest workers and crosses the River Duror which flows in from the east. The Auchindarroch Caravan Park is passed where there were sidings.

The railway trackbed then draws closer to the road as the valley narrows on the approach to Kentallen. The trackbed loses height and enters a deep cutting with worsening conditions underfoot before reaching the site of the rail bridge over the road, which has been removed. The last section before Kentallen Station is by the loch side.

Holiday chalets have been constructed over the platforms at Kentallen (013583) and the station building extended to become the Holly Tree Hotel. The wooden lamp hut at Kentallen now graces Birkhill Platform on the Bo'ness and Kinneil Railway. Houses have been built immediately to the north of the station, blocking the trackbed, but the trackbed soon resumes its coastal path turning round the northern tip of the Appin peninsula towards the mouth of Loch Leven. After Ballachulish Pier the railway turned inland passing under the road and passing behind what is now Gragons Touth Golf Course and

Kentallen looking to Connel Ferry, with old camping coach and 'Matisa' ballast tamping machine

Ballachulish House before heading towards the coast again and the site of Ballachulish Ferry Station (053594). Passengers would alight at the station to take the short ferry trip across Loch Leven at this narrow point. The curved concrete platform of the station is found to the west of the approach road to the Ballachulish Bridge, opened in 1975, which now cuts across the trackbed and removed the need for the ferry crossing or the alternative - a long road detour by Kinlochleven. Landscaping on the bridge approaches has removed the trackbed and between here and Ballachulish Station there are only glimpses of it remaining. This was the site of the bridge too far for the WHR proposed route from Fort William, which was opposed by the quarry owners.

The final approach to Ballachulish Station has been converted to a road and the station building itself survives as a medical centre. The terminus had two bays with a goods yard to the north of the station. Behind the former station site is a towering quarry face, a reminder of one of the main revenue sources for the first few years of the line's existence. The station underwent several name changes starting as Ballachulish, then Ballachulish and Glencoe in 1905 and then Ballachulish (Glencoe) for Kinlochleven in 1908. Until the end of the First World War there was no road route down the west side of Loch Leven to the aluminium smelter at Kinlochleven from Ballachulish and only a drove road on the east side. At this time steam ships brought men, if they didn't walk, and raw materials to Kinlochleven.

Kinlochleven had several industrial railways while the aluminium smelter was being constructed or in use: a line from the pier to the aluminium factory - the pier circular walk now enables anyone to follow the route of this short branch and enjoy the views down Loch Leven. On the hills behind Kinlochleven

Ballachulish 1956

were located the hydroelectric dams which supplied the power to the smelter plant. Several lines were constructed to carry materials, including an aerial railway, where heavy iron buckets were hung from steel cables, which ran for five miles from the pier to the dam. This type of arrangement was known as a 'Blondin'. One local story tells of how the packman, who sold goods to the workmen of dubious quality and at inflated prices, was encouraged to expand his business by taking a lift on one of the iron buckets up to the dam to sell his wares one Saturday. Not realising the workmens' loathing of his exploitation he clambered in and started the journey. The 'Blondin' stopped at midday on Saturday, while he was enroute, and he was stuck in the bucket until the Monday much to the satisfaction of the workmen!

Further south of Ballachulish near the mouth of Loch Leven is the village of Glen Coe and the towering hills at the entrance to Glen Coe, the site of the infamous massacre of the Macdonalds by the Campbells, under the King's orders, in 1692. Tourists travelled on the train before the road connections through the glen improved in the 1930s, marvelling at the beauty of the glen and helping to sustain, for a time, five trains a day on the route.

The Ballachulish Branch was one of the most scenic lines in Scotland and made a remote peninsula accessible. Today with sections being used as a cycle path the route's popularity will increase, even if the mode of transport has changed, and more people will enjoy the scenic pleasures offered by the

Ballachulish Ferry looking to Connel Ferry 1956

trackbed of this remote branch line. John Anderson may have lost a lot of goodwill with some of his decisions when the line opened but the legacies of the line will more than make up for it.

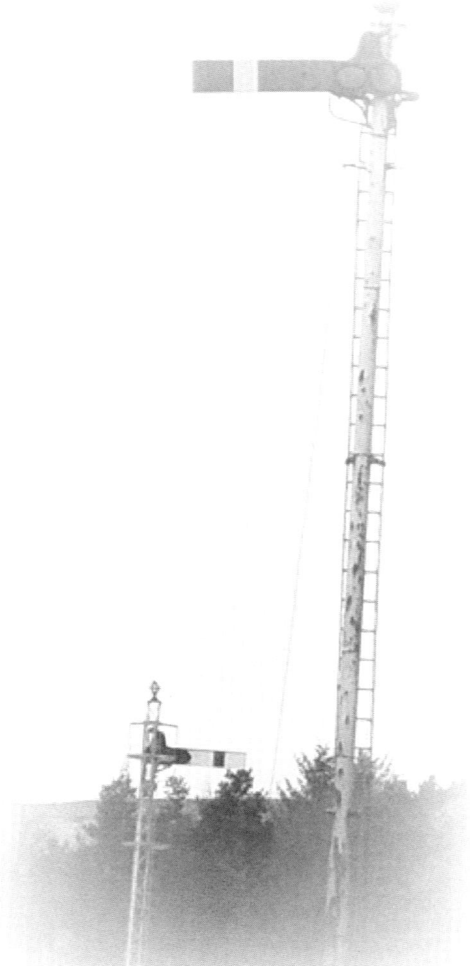

Chapter Three

Loch Lomond and the Trossachs

Rails to Aberfoyle and the Forth and Clyde Junction Railway

Rails to Aberfoyle:
'Royal Romances, Decimal Points and Fairies'

The journey from Glasgow (Queen Street) to Aberfoyle involved travelling not on one railway but five, and must have been a challenge for the accountants who had to allocate receipts among the various companies. The first railway used was part of the Glasgow to Edinburgh mainline, whose route was used as far as Lenzie. From Lenzie Junction the route to Aberfoyle diverged using four local railways, one in part, to reach Aberfoyle. One of the railways, the Forth and Clyde Junction Railway (F&CJR) already existed, stretching from Stirling to Loch Lomond and is described later in this chapter and only a short section of its route was used. The other three railways were small rural branches which eventually linked up to reach Aberfoyle. There was no grand plan, it almost seemed as if the railway arrived by accident at Aberfoyle.

Aberfoyle as a destination was worthy of consideration situated at the 'Gateway to the Trossachs' and with large quarries nearby to add extra revenue. The village, however, turned out to be not the tourist magnet hoped for, at least in railway days, and passenger numbers soon dropped off although goods traffic from the slate quarries at Aberfoyle sustained the route for a while. Regular commuters tempted to use the railway to reach Glasgow, an important part of the companies' proposed business plan, also had to endure a very indirect route and that was the problem. A scenic line, the railway simply couldn't compete when the roads improved. Indeed it was just over thirty-four miles from Glasgow to Aberfoyle by railway.

The route started at Lenzie Junction, already eight miles east of Glasgow. There it left the main Edinburgh to Glasgow route, travelled north through the industrial town of Kirkintilloch, passing under the Forth and Clyde canal, then west along the southern flanks of the Campsie Fells. It now wound its way north, across the farm lands and peat bogs of the Forth Valley, towards the hills of the Trossachs looming above Aberfoyle. The route, from Lenzie Junction, was opened in sections, built by three different railway companies but each eventually operated by the NBR. The Campsie Branch, which opened in 1848, ran between Lenzie Junction and Lennoxtown (Old) and was built for the Edinburgh and Glasgow Railway (E&GR) (later taken over by the NBR). The Campsie Branch was double track but beyond Lennoxtown the route was single track. The Blane Valley Railway (BVR) operated between a new station in Lennoxtown to Killearn and opened in 1866 and the route was finally extended north, in 1882, to reach Aberfoyle by the Strathendrick and Aberfoyle Railway (S&AR). Part of this last section, between Gartness Junction and Buchlyvie, was shared with the F&CJR, which had opened in 1856.

The BVR and the S&AR were both taken over by the NBR in 1891, and having had a timetable and high fares imposed on them, the NBR found poorly equipped railways with inadequate facilities. They upgraded the route and attempted to raise staff morale with competitions such as 'the best kept station award'. This certainly involved the locals who were known 'to lend' the station plants to improve displays on the day of inspection. Initially the railway was the only means of transport for many who lived along its route but in time it was badly affected by competition from the car and buses. A very restricted service operated on the line and the passenger service 'died' in 1951 and freight eight years later. Local industry around Kirkintilloch and from print works at Milton of Campsie, Lennoxtown and Blanefield along with farming and tourism provided some income for the line as did coal deliveries. The Campsie Branch survived only a few years longer, with services on the route stopped completely for passengers by 1966.

While Aberfoyle was viewed as a railway terminus with progress north blocked by the hills, some early plans proposed railways extending from or near Aberfoyle to Crianlarich as part of the quest for a route to the Western Highlands. The Glasgow and North Western Railway, in 1882, the year the railway reached Aberfoyle, proposed a railway from Glasgow up the east coast of Loch Lomond and hence by Glen Falloch, Crianlarich, Fort William and the Great Glen to Inverness, reducing the journey to Inverness, by forty-two miles over the existing route via Perth. While the NBR considered the plans, the CR and HR combined to defeat the proposals. At the same time the S&AR proposed an extension through Aberfoyle to Crianlarich but this soon, not surprisingly, failed. An earlier third route via Aberfoyle, Loch Katrine and hence Glen Falloch to Crianlarich was put forward by the Caledonian Northern Direct Railway, who claimed CR backing, but this also came to nothing.

Exploring the Railway Heritage

The route in this section is covered by the following maps:
Explorer 342, 347, 348, 365

There were stations on the route at Kirkintilloch (8 miles from Glasgow (Queen Street)), Milton of Campsie (9.75 miles), Lennoxtown (11.5 miles), Campsie Glen (12.5 miles), Strathblane (15.75 miles), Blanefield (16.75 miles), Dumgoyne (18.75 miles), Killearn (21.25 miles), Buchlyvie (F&C 28.5 miles), Gartmore (32.5 miles) and Aberfoyle (34.25 miles).

There are few remains of the railway left between Lenzie Junction and Kirkintilloch Station. From Lenzie Junction (originally known as Campsie Junction) (660721) where the route left the Glasgow to Edinburgh route it is easy to confuse the trackbed of the Monkland and Kirkintilloch Railway with the Campsie Branch as both lines ran close together and only sections of each remain. The first station on the route Back O'Loch Halt, which only opened in 1925, and was situated in a deep cutting, has disappeared and an access road will soon pass through the site.

From Kirkintilloch to Gartness the trackbed is generally in good condition. The route is signposted as the Strathkelvin Walkway between Kirkintilloch and Strathblane. At Dumgoyach Hill, north of Blanefield, the West Highland Way joins the trackbed as far as Gartness. Between Gartness and Buchlyvie is described in the section on the F&CJR but is generally in poor condition. Between Buchlyvie and Aberfoyle is part of National Cycle Route No.7 with the trackbed in good condition.

Campsie Branch

The best starting point is in Kirkintilloch to the north of the A803 where an abutment of a rail bridge (655744) indicates the start of a walkway along the route. A short distance south of the road was Kirkintilloch Station, of which nothing survives, the site occupied by the Campsie View Nursing Home. On the southern approach to Kirkintilloch Station the railway passed under Hillhead aqueduct carrying the Forth and Clyde Canal. It is worth backtracking to view this feat of engineering as the Luggie Water also passes under the canal and the railway, at the aqueduct, before reaching the River Kelvin.

The 'unique bridge' showing the Campsie Branch railway passing under the Forth and Clyde Canal and Luggie Water passing under both the railway and canal (1924)

Heading north towards Milton of Campsie the route crossed the River Kelvin just to the west of where the Glazert Water joined it. The rail bridge has been replaced by a footbridge. To the right, at the rail bridge, are the now closed Broomhill and Lanfine Hospitals. Broomhill catered for patients with incurable illnesses and opened in 1874 and Lanfine opened in 1904 to look after those suffering from tuberculosis. The hospitals closed in 1995 and at present stand derelict.

After the bridge the trackbed stays close to the west bank of the Glazert Water until it reaches Milton of Campsie Station. En route it passed under the Kelvin Valley Railway (KVR), (Maryhill, Glasgow to Kilsyth) (658753). The KVR required a 120 foot long, four arch bridge to cross both the Campsie Branch and the Glazert Water. The arch of the bridge crossing the Campsie Branch has been removed. Just to the south of the bridge the concrete foundations of the bridge (Kelvin Valley West Junction) which carried a short spur between the Campsie Branch and the KVR can be seen in the river bed. The KVR was described as an amateurish organisation outwitted by the NBR who exploited it. The Kelvin Valley West Junction allowed coal from pits near Kilsyth, to the east, to reach Lenzie and onto the Clyde for export. The section of the KVR west of the Campsie Branch was left underdeveloped for most of its existence.

As the trackbed turns west on the approach to the Milton of Campsie Station there were sidings to the left serving the Kincaid Print Works, the first of several calico print works on this branch. The station (652768) lies to the east of the road bridge which carries the B757 over the former railway. The

Milton of Campsie looking west 1954

platforms remain intact, and extend both sides of the road bridge, but the buildings have been removed. The road bridge has been reinforced with the arch reduced in size and lined with corrugated metal. From its opening in 1874 until 1912, the station was simply known as Milton.

The trackbed continues further west to Lennoxtown along the foothills of the Campsie Fells, where the route initially stopped. The trackbed crossed the Glazert Water no fewer than three times. The first crossing uses a new bridge. On this section were sidings to the north, bridging the Glazert Water to access the Lilyburn Print Works and on the left beyond the B822, where there was

Milton of Campsie Station site

a level crossing at Rowantreefauld Cottages and beyond is the second bridge over the Glazert Water, followed, shortly, by a rail bridge over a minor road. Sidings served the Underwood Chemical Works and the Campsie Alum Works to the south.

When the railway was extended west a new Lennoxtown Station was opened and the original station became the town's goods station. The final rail bridge over the Glazert Water on the approach to the first Lennoxtown Station is blocked and the rail bridge built over the river, when the line was extended towards Strathblane, has been removed. There is an easy detour to the left which leads to Station Road just south of a road bridge over the river and the railway.

Originally the railway stopped in Lennoxtown to the east of Station Road. Sidings fanned out to each side of the station with an extension into the now demolished Lennoxtown Print Works, which were located to the west of Station Road. The siding crossed Station Road at a level crossing. A mill dam on the north of the main street, which still exists, supplied the works. The original station site has been landscaped and is now occupied by sports facilities. An industrial estate has been built on the site of the former print works with a housing development extending to the former railway trackbed.

The area was renowned for its 'printed calico' or Indian cotton. The cotton was first treated with substances like sour milk or urine and left to bleach in the sun before being printed in bright colours. Dams were built to collect the water used in the processes. The Glazert Water was greatly discoloured by the pollution produced by the works but has now recovered. The mills closed in 1929 and the site was eventually taken over by the 'Kali' nail company from 1941 until 1972.

Lennoxtown 1950

The alum works used a discovery made by the Romans that if cloths were first dipped in alum solution before dying then the dye would adhere better to the surface of the cloth. To the south of Lennoxtown were several small coal and limestone mines which helped supply the works with raw materials. The alum works were managed for a time by Charles Macintosh, famous for the development of waterproof fabrics and the 'Macintosh coat'.

The new station in Lennoxtown, known as Lennoxtown (Blane Valley) for the first fourteen years, eventually becoming known simply as Lennoxtown, was located to the east of the two arch overbridge on Station Road close to the banks of the river. A pipeline laid along this stretch of trackbed has removed all traces of the station. The station, on the town side of the track, was of brick construction with a short wooden canopy. There was a signal box on the eastern approaches to control access to the goods station, Lennoxtown (Old).

Blane Valley Railway

The eroded volcanic rocks of the Campsie Fells dominate Lennoxtown. Rising steeply, their mood seems reflected on the town nestling at their foot. Clouds bring gloom, reflected sunshine brightens the town. To the railway builders, however, the Campsie Fells were an impenetrable barrier. The only way was around them, and that was the route taken by the BVR. To Glaswegians the Campsies formed part of the hills to the north of the city with the distinctive hump of Dumgoyne a well known landmark. To reach the Campsies represented escape from the tenements and the deprivation of a Victorian city. So despite the industrial nature of this section the railway attracted many day trippers wanting to picnic in the countryside beside the Campsie Fells, easily accessed from the stations. Extra trains were provided to cope with the demand around the turn of the twentieth century.

Looking west from close to the overbridge at the former station site, Lennox Castle can be seen. Also west of the overbridge the trackbed continues along the tree lined banks of the Glazert Water at the start of the Blane Valley route. A few hundred yards along the trackbed, opposite Balglass Farm on the southern bank of the river was a loop siding into the Lennoxtown Print Works.

The route then passes through a wooded area and under an elaborate overbridge, before the entrance to the extensive grounds of Lennox Castle is reached. The castle was designed by the architect David Hamilton in 1837. It is a Grade A listed building and has been damaged by fire. The castle was used as a military hospital in both wars and as a maternity unit which opened in 1944. A siding was built into the grounds, during the First World War, and the railway brought in both wounded and supplies. The site expanded when it became a mental institution for up to 1200 patients in 1936. During the Second World War the patients were transferred to 'temporary huts' which were used for the next forty years! The castle was used as a hostel for the nursing staff. Strict segregation of male and females was practised both for patients and staff.

The hospital was closed in 2002 and the hospital buildings demolished. Some of the grounds were bought by Celtic Football Club and have been developed as a modern training facility which opened in 2007. There are also plans for house building on the site.

Campsie Glen Station (614787) is located near the entrance. The platform to the north of the line remains in a crumbling state amongst trees. The trackbed then reaches more open countryside, still overlooked by the Campsie Fells. The Glazert Water having tumbled down the steep slopes of the Campsie Fells passes under the trackbed at this point. It is joined by the Fin Glen Burn which in spate can be also be seen plummeting down the narrow Fin Glen etched out of the slopes of the Campsie Fells. In the increasingly narrow valley, with rising moorland to the south, the trackbed edges closer to the Strathblane Road and the Campsie Fells. Ahead is the distinctive Dunglass Hill, the eroded remains of the basalt rock plug of an old volcano. A siding was built to remove materials quarried from the hill.

Beyond the hill the trackbed enters a deep cutting on the approach to Strathblane Station and the walker is forced onto the A891 just before the station site (564792). The trackbed now continues through the landscaped

Strathblane 1951

gardens of what looks like the station master's cottage before reaching a brick abutment of a rail bridge over the A81. Road realignment means that the abutment is lost amongst trees. The original rail bridge was stolen, its metal work proving too tempting. More surprisingly no one noticed assuming that the thieves were part of the official demolition team! The stolen metal work was never retrieved.

The detour onto the A891 leads past the Kirkhouse Inn. Turning right onto the A81 for a few hundred yards the road on the left, leading to the primary school, should be taken. Beyond the school are playing fields and at the north end on higher ground the trackbed can be found. From the 'stolen railway bridge' the railway originally passed through Strathblane on an embankment. What is left of the embankment now starts beyond the playing fields. To the right of the trackbed is the pipe track from Loch Katrine which passed underneath the railway and whose water supplies Glasgow. Also to the right was the Blanefield Print Works on the far side of the Blane Water. Blanefield Station (550793) was situated just before the narrow twisting B821 Stockiemuir Road. Station cottages exist next to the road where there was a level crossing. The simple narrow wooden station building, on an island platform has been removed. Passengers transferred onto the train for Aberfoyle at Blanefield Station. There was a goods shed, sidings and a loading bank beside the station. The loading bank can still be seen to the right (looking towards Aberfoyle).

Due to further pipes being laid along the trackbed, part of the Loch Lomond Water Supply Scheme, sections of the embankment have been removed and it is difficult to recognise the site as a railway trackbed. The conditions underfoot at Blanefield Station and on the next section are poor because drainage has

Blanefield 1950

been damaged by the pipe laying. The attractive villages of Strathblane and Blanefield, long merged into one, are popular residences for those wishing to live on the outskirts of Glasgow. The villages are overlooked by the steep slopes of the Strathblane Hills, on the western edge of the Campsie Fells. Part of the Monty Python movie *The Meaning of Life* was filmed on these hills, overlooking the villages. From the villages it is a short journey by road (A81), initially up a steep hill, to reach the outskirts of Glasgow. The long detour via Lenzie forced on the railway by the contours of the land meant that the railway was always disadvantaged.

Across the steeply climbing Stockiemuir Road the trackbed continues, sharing its route with the water pipeline until the next station at Dumgoyne and at one point what could be mistaken for a loading bay is actually an inspection portal for the pipeline. For the next mile the trackbed is lined with trees, with the Blane Water to the right. Duntreath Castle, the home of the Edmonstone family for nearly six hundred years, is across the Blane Water. Here King Edward VII was entertained and rumours of a royal romance, fuelled by easy access to the castle from the railway, were strong and probably true! The gardens and pond of the castle are well maintained and can be glimpsed between the trees that fringe the trackbed and while there have been changes one can still imagine grand Edwardian parties on the terraces and lawns of the house.

To the left of the track bed is the rounded and wooded Dumgoyach Hill. Beyond the hill the trackbed crosses the Blane Water by a single arch bridge with wing walls to reach a gate. From the left, the West Highland Way, a ninety-five mile long distance footpath between Milngavie, to the north of Glasgow, and Fort William, joins. Until Gartness, the West Highland Way shares the trackbed of the former railway. On a summer's day the trackbed can be very busy carrying more passengers than the railway usually did.

Almost immediately the views towards the Campsie Fells improve, with the 1404 foot Dumgoyne, a forty million year old volcanic plug, on the western edge of the Campsie Fells prominent. The trackbed reaches more open ground with increasing views in the direction of Aberfoyle, the terminus of the railway still over fifteen miles away, and the Trossachs.

At the base of Dumgoyne lies Glengoyne Distillery with its warehouses stretching towards the trackbed. All distilleries need a good supply of water and Glengoyne obtains its supply from the hill and collects it in a reservoir behind the distillery. Set back from an old drover's road, the whisky could be distilled in secret hidden from travellers and yet still close to Glasgow. Rob Roy, the well-known cattle thief roamed these lands, stealing cattle and returning them only on payment of a ransom. Given that the cattle they stole were usually black in colour, this gave rise to the term 'blackmail'. Rob Roy wasn't always successful and was once forced to hide in an old tree a few hundred yards from the site of the distillery. Myths abound about whisky distilleries; one is that the Highland Boundary Fault line runs along the road in front of the distillery meaning that while the whisky is distilled in the Highlands it is left to mature in the Lowlands across the road, on the railway side. The Highland Boundary Fault Line is in fact further north at Aberfoyle. There is some truth in the story but it is not the Highland Boundary Fault Line that divides the distillery but an imaginary line that divides the Highland and Lowland whisky regions. In such an attractive setting close to Glasgow and near the Trossachs the distillery is a popular tourist attraction.

I did not visit the distillery when I lived in the nearby village of Killearn, although I have recently and it does produce a gentle, and for some, the attraction of an unpeated dram! More important to me was the memory of this particular stretch of old railway. Inspired by the writings of John Thomas and his book on *Forgotten Railways: Scotland*, borrowed on a whim from the local library I walked along the trackbed, with my first son strapped to my back to search for the remains of Blanefield Station and to give my wife respite from the incessant demands of an active youngster. A picture of the station in the 1930's and one of the Royal trains paying a visit to the area helped fire my imagination. John Thomas, sadly no longer with us, remains one of Scotland's finest writers on railway history, a fine chronicler of lost railways. It would be appropriate to toast him with a small dram of seventeen year old Glengoyne.

Shortly after the whisky warehouses are passed the trackbed approaches the site of Dumgoyne Station, where two station cottages have been transformed

Dumgoyne looking to Glasgow 1957

into the popular Beech Tree Inn, a favourite with walkers on the West Highland Way. Originally the station was known as Killearn when the BVR terminated here and then Killearn Old (1882) when the line was extended. In 1896 it became known as Dumgoyne Hill and then simply Dumgoyne in 1897. The station buildings, to the left of the cottages, have been demolished. Beyond the station the railway crossed the road at an angle by a level crossing. Whisky casks from Glengoyne were loaded on goods wagons and delivered by rail to the blenders in Glasgow, giving a distinct advantage to the distillery over more isolated distilleries.

Strathendrick and Aberfoyle Railway

The West Highland Way continues to the right of the A81 closely following the trackbed of the former railway. The village of Killearn is to the right on the slopes of the Campsies. On this stretch was another hospital, Killearn Hospital commissioned by the Government prior to the outbreak of war and completed in 1940. It cared for both military and civilian casualties and at peak had over 600 beds. The hospital consisted of prefabricated buildings spread over the grounds. After the war the hospital specialised in orthopaedics and neurosurgery before closing in 1972. Hospital visitors had until 1951 the option of visiting by train. The site has since lain unused apart from a brief appearance in an episode of the police series about the Glasgow policeman *Taggart*.

The area was also earmarked to house the world famous 'Burrell collection'. Given that many of the items in the collection were very vulnerable to atmospheric pollution, the clean air of Killearn was strongly considered as the terms of Burrell's bequest stalled the construction of a home for his collection, due to air pollution, in Glasgow. Long after the 'Clean Air Act' had taken effect, it was finally agreed that Pollok Estate in Glasgow was a more suitable and central site.

The site of Killearn New Station (509853) is found on the north side of the B834. It became known as Killearn in 1896. Neither Killearn Station was particularly convenient for the villagers. The laying of a pipe track has removed signs of the station. Further on the trackbed reaches the A81. The road bridge over the trackbed has been filled in but the trackbed continues on the far side stopping at a road bridge over the line on the approach to Gartness. Beyond the bridge the trackbed disappears, ploughed into a field, although on the north side of the field the southern abutment of the demolished rail bridge over the Endrick Water can be seen. Gartness Junction, where it joined the F&CJR lies to the north of the River Endrick. Follow the signs for the

Killearn 1951

West Highland Way a short distance until the village of Gartness is reached. Through the village, crossing the road bridge, takes the walker to the former site of the level crossing over the road where the trackbed can be rejoined. The West Highland Way then continues west towards Drymen and the banks of Loch Lomond.

A series of rocky pools at Gartness known as the Pots of Gartness are a good place to watch salmon jumping. This small hamlet was also part of the estate of John Napier, a philosopher and mathematician, born in Edinburgh, who lived in the sixteenth century and invented logarithms which simplified complex calculations which led, among other advances, to the development of Newton's theory of gravity. He introduced the decimal point as a way of expressing fractions, something which many school pupils must have regretted. His contribution to many different fields, he also invented a hydraulic pump, is not widely recognised, partly because his main interest lay in theology and everything else was a hobby. He lived close to the waterfall and mill in Gartness. The latter sometimes disturbed him when he was deep in thought and he would ask the miller to stop. With a pet black cockerel and often seeming distracted, some locals were alarmed by his eccentricity and rumours circulated about him being in league with dark forces. However, today his genius is widely recognised and Napier University in Edinburgh is named after him.

Forth and Clyde Junction Railway

A description of the trackbed between Gartness Junction and Buchlyvie Junction is given in the next section on the Forth and Clyde Junction Railway.

Buchlyvie Junction to Aberfoyle

From Buchlyvie Station the railway crossed the B835 by a level crossing. The trackbed, double track for the short section to Buchlyvie Junction, is carried on a high embankment crossing a minor road before reaching the junction. This short section was doubled when the Aberfoyle branch opened. The bridge over the minor road was widened with the addition of a brick lined arch. Buchlyvie Junction is north of the village and east of the station. The Aberfoyle branch veered north-east before turning to head north-west towards Aberfoyle, crossing the soft mossy ground of the Carse of Stirling towards the Menteith Hills, looming to the north of the undulating plain. Almost immediately the trackbed now enters woodland and continues in a straight line, crossing first the Kelty Water and then the River Forth as it makes its way across Flanders Moss, part of the Carse of Stirling. When the railway was built there was no forest just a peat bog. The soft spongy landscape was made capable of taking the weight of the trains by laying brushwood mats along the proposed line until a firm base was created. Even so the weight of the trains must have caused the land to vibrate. It is suggested that the name Flanders came from the Scots word 'flinders', meaning to shake or tremble and, particularly, when the trains were crossing the Moss this would have seemed an appropriate term.

Double bridge showing the addition of the brick-lined arch

The route across Flanders Moss is quiet and secluded with glimpses of distant hills through gaps in the woods. The trackbed emerges from the woods near the bridges which cross first the Auchentroig Burn and then the Kelty Water. The bridges have been upgraded.

Due to a lack of foresight, the Forestry Commission did not buy back from the local farmer the bowstring girder bridge over the River Forth, which they had previously sold to him, not realising its value, and the bridge was sold for scrap. Fortunately the missing link has been restored and a new footbridge, Gartrenich Bridge, now spans the River Forth. Using a wooden walkway bolted onto a metal girder frame and the abutments of the old railway bridge, the bridge also provides another route for those walking or cycling between Buchlyvie and Aberfoyle. The bridge is considerably less famous and imposing than its illustrious cousin down river.

Over the bridge the trackbed continues and soon reaches the site of Gartmore Station

The new Gartrenich Bridge

(533986). The station originally lay to the right of the A81 but road realignment has changed this arrangement and the site of the station now lies to the west of the new skewed-arch concrete bridge which carries the realigned road. Apart from a privately owned station cottage nothing remains of the station. The station had a basic ticket office and waiting room but all signs of the station have been removed. The station had a fleeting moment of fame when it was used as a location in the 1955 film *Geordie* about a boy who follows a postal body building course and eventually reaches the Olympic Games. He, along with his girlfriend, leave the train at the station and in the next scene appears on the slopes of Loch Ard many miles to the north. If only trains could have been so efficient at transporting people! The locals were disappointed that having renovated the station, the film company changed its appearance to make it look rundown and changed the name to Drumfechan. The Scottish scenes in *Geordie* were all filmed in the Trossachs. Beside the station site is a concrete pill box dating from the Second World War. Well positioned it covers both the road (original alignment) and the railway, so if the enemy came either by road or across Flanders Moss, using the railway trackbed, their advance was covered. Thankfully it wasn't used.

Gartmore, renamed 'Drumfechan' for filming, 1954

    The village of Gartmore is about a mile away on a sloping hillside overlooking the Stirling valley. It was built in the late eighteenth century as a planned village. Visible on the hillside is Gartmore House, surrounded by woods. Built by the Grahams, the house remained in their ownership until the time of Robert Cunninghame Graham, writer and politician, who was the co-founder of the Scottish Labour Party and first president of the Scottish National Party. Nowadays it is a Christian conference centre and is used for activity holidays.

Military pillbox near Gartmore Station

Beyond the former station site the trackbed turns towards Aberfoyle, then enters a deep cutting and passes under a minor road, leading out of Gartmore. The bridge has been filled in but the new path is well signposted. Beyond this point, until Aberfoyle, the trackbed becomes a tarmacked walkway. The trackbed passes Doon Hill to the left of the walkway on the approach to Aberfoyle. The hill forms part of Aberfoyle's claim to be the fairy capital of Scotland. The Reverend Robert Kirk, a noted scholar, and minister at Aberfoyle, wrote about many subjects including fairies. He visited the tree clad Doon Hill, known locally as the fairy knoll, daily and died of a heart attack on its slopes. Locals claim that he was spirited away by the fairies and didn't really die!

To the right of the trackbed is the A821 and to its right are the steep wooded slopes at the edge of the Menteith Hills. For the final mile the railway was leaving the flat plain of the upper Forth Valley and entering the Highlands. Aberfoyle lies on the Highland Boundary Fault where the mountainous Highlands and the Lowlands of the south collide. A row of station cottages is reached and then a bridge crosses a stream and passes through a small wood before the walkway ends, disappointingly, at a car park. This was the site of Aberfoyle Station (522009), now part of the car park for the Scottish Wool Centre. The station had a single platform with engine shed, terminus and sidings. The curved edge stones of the turntable pit can be found amongst the trees. There was also a connection with the tramway from the local quarry.

Aberfoyle, as a railway destination, was promoted with high hopes as a gateway to the Trossachs and Loch Katrine and it is still advertised as such, long after the last train has left. The Trossachs were originally thought of as

Aberfoyle looking to Dead End 1957

the area between Loch Katrine and Loch Achray to the east, but has now become part of the larger Loch Lomond and Trossachs National Park. The Duke's Pass road (A821) was built by the Duke of Montrose in 1882, on the arrival of the railway, to link Aberfoyle to the southern end of Loch Katrine and to allow the hills and glens to be explored. The four and a half mile road climbs and twists, providing stunning views, but was initially a private toll road with no cars allowed. It was improved and became toll-free in the 1930s. The road continues east towards Callander. Near the top of the hill overlooking Aberfoyle is the David Marshall Lodge, the visitor centre for the Queen Elizabeth Forest Park. Forests now clothe much of the land around Aberfoyle. The views from the centre, particularly over the Forth Valley towards the Campsie Fells, give a good overview of the route taken by the railway but dramatic views extend in all directions.

The area is steeped in romantic associations by the works of Sir Walter Scott and William Wordsworth. Popularised during the nineteenth century, as one of the haunts of Rob Roy it was hoped that Aberfoyle might attract day trippers eager for an outing to the edge of the Highlands to explore the wonderful diversity of scenery.

One of the important lochs in the Trossachs is Loch Katrine which has supplied Glasgow with pure water since 1859. Earlier Sir Walter Scott's poem *The Lady of the Lake* brought the public's attention to the loch and even Queen Victoria sailed on it. There are still sailings on the loch using the Steamship *Sir Walter Scott*.

The forests help to cover the scars left by the once extensive slate and limestone quarries, around Aberfoyle. The quarries were big enough to have their own railway networks and the slate quarry at Craigmore, to the west of the A821, involved a steep incline (one in eight) and a drop in height of almost 750 feet to link up with the railway at Aberfoyle Station. The bottom of the incline was located behind the school house in Aberfoyle. The quarries were open for almost two hundred years and finally closed in 1958. The mineral railway was closed only in 1947. The David Marshall Lodge is built of local slate to reflect the area's past. Some of the forest trails around the lodge include sections of the old tramways.

Aberfoyle is no longer associated with quarrying or the railway and forestry has developed as the major local industry. However it is the natural and often dramatic beauty of the Trossachs combined with a romantic and interesting history which still attracts the visitors. The fairies knew what they were doing when they inhabited this area!

The Forth and Clyde Junction Railway

'Hopes and Dreams'

The Forth and Clyde Junction Railway (F&CJR) seemed like a good idea, a link between Scotland's two major rivers, providing another route for goods to be transported to the docks. Linking up with two other proposed railways would enable traffic to flow between the Rivers Forth and Clyde. Those promoting the railway imagined that it would provide an alternative route for the export of commodities like coal, slate, lime and agricultural products. It was also hoped that the route would be used by importers to transport commodities like flour from Canada and sugar from the West Indies across Scotland. Textiles from the Vale of Leven could also be carried east and exported to the continent from the Forth ports. The route also had the additional attraction of opening up the Trossachs and Loch Lomond area to tourists. It appeared, therefore, to have considerably more potential than many other routes touted during the boom years of railway development. The promoters were entitled to their hopes and dreams.

Raising sufficient money locally was a problem since the area was so lightly populated – fewer than ten thousand people lived in the area around the route. Rivals certainly believed in the dream, but to them it was a potential nightmare. Those running the Edinburgh and Glasgow Railway (E&GR) and the Forth and Clyde canal who owned existing cross-country routes, which would be in direct competition to the F&CJR, invested in the proposed share capital of the company. Since local interests could not provide sufficient funding for the venture, this allowed for manipulation of the share capital by those likely to suffer a loss in their business by the opening of the railway. They used their voting power to narrowly win a vote scrapping the parliamentary bill in 1846 and stopping the railway going ahead. At this time the proposed railways, at the eastern and western ends of the F&CJR, which linked to the rivers, were not ready. At the eastern end the SCR, between Greenhill Junction and Perth did not open until 1850, and it was 1852 before the Caledonian and Dunbartonshire Railway (C&DR) opened at the western end.

The C&DR ran between Bowling, on the River Clyde and Balloch at the western end of the F&CJR. There was a link to Glasgow but this was by steamer not railway. The C&DR operated sailings between Glasgow and Bowling with passengers then travelling by train through the Vale of Leven to reach Balloch. Bowling was situated where the Forth and Clyde canal joined the River Clyde and could attract trade from each but there was little room for expansion of the port facilities. With no direct rail link to Glasgow the F&CJR could compete for all the business in the Vale of Leven and trade through Bowling, but this advantage did not last for long.

Just over seven years later, in 1852, a second bill was presented to parliament seeking less capital but again emphasizing the potential of the line. This time the proposal succeeded and by January 1854 the first sod was cut near Stirling. The thirty mile long route branched from the then SCR, just north of Stirling Station, wound round the north of Stirling Castle and headed west through the flat farming land of the Carse of Stirling. Engineering works were light, with only the bridging of the River Endrick, east of Drymen Station, requiring significant construction and even here costs were reduced by building a wooden viaduct. The River Leven was also crossed by a modest bridge near to the western terminus at Balloch. Otherwise the carefully chosen route required only crossing of streams and a few roads. Level crossings were used where possible to further reduce costs. The highest point on the line, only 230 feet, was between Buchlyvie and Gartness. The route was single track, although enough land was purchased to double this if required. It wasn't and in many sections the route looked like a fenced country lane.

One problem typical of the railways built at this time was that the railway station was frequently some distance from the community served. Port of Menteith station was four miles from the community it served and both Balfron and Drymen stations two miles away from their communities. In the flat Carse of Stirling the villages were often built on high ground to allow for drainage while the railway used the lower ground, to avoid additional construction costs. Villagers often were forced to walk some distance to use the railway and with the introduction of buses and cars the railways lost out.

The development of the route was also not helped by the removal from the original plans of a proposed extension to Milngavie, on the outskirts of Glasgow, by a branch starting near Drymen. This failed to make the final parliamentary bill, much to the disappointment of many supporters, ensuring that those travelling to Glasgow had an inconvenient and circuitous route by Balloch or later by the BVR. The circuitous route also affected other parts of the business. Initially farmers used the line to send milk to the Glasgow area but with the opening of the BVR in 1866 this business declined; farmers switched to the BVR line which, itself, was hardly the most direct. When buses started to offer competition, with their direct routes into Glasgow, the F&CJR also suffered badly.

When the F&CJR scheme was revived, running rights over the SCR, the C&DR and also the Stirling and Dunfermline Railway were obtained and a route between the two rivers was finally secured. Like most railways the F&CJR wanted to be independent and reap the profits. For the first year of its existence the SCR provided engines and crews for F&CJR but a dispute over charging brought this arrangement to an end and the F&CJR went it alone. By 1865, however, the CR and NBR both sought control over the F&CJR in order to control the considerable summer tourist traffic to Loch Lomond. Even at this early stage hopes of coal and other commodities being transported by this route were diminishing due to the development of more direct routes through Glasgow in which the NBR had invested money. With the Forth and Clyde canal also suffering from the railway competition, and the upper reaches of the River Clyde becoming more accessible to larger boats, Bowling did not develop as a major port, further hampering the prospects of the F&CJR.

The interest of the NBR in the F&CJR developed through a series of expansions and takeovers. The Caledonian and Dunbartonshire Railway had reached Loch Lomond in 1850. However by 1858 another railway the Glasgow, Dumbarton and Helensburgh Railway was opened, allowing for the first time a rail route from Glasgow along the north bank of the Clyde. The two railways shared a section of track and formed a joint committee. In 1862 they were both absorbed by the E&GR and in 1865 by the NBR. Thus the NBR had at last achieved one of their strategic aims, a route along the north bank of the River Clyde which, they hoped, could compete with the CR for coastal traffic on the river. They then made the first move for the F&CJR to secure the traffic in the Vale of Leven and the Loch Lomond tourist trade, but this was rejected.

The CR had acquired the SCR in 1865 and was also keen to reach Loch Lomond, from the east, but their offer was similarly rejected by the directors of the F&CJR. Stirling Council backed the CR bid, fearing that the NBR would reduce the F&CJR to a little used rural line and not allow the CR access to Loch Lomond. Their concerns were well founded. A fierce battle between the NBR and CR continued while the F&CJR struggled, trying to generate business in a sparsely populated area, until eventually in 1871 the NBR emerged victorious, concluding a thirty year agreement which was increased to fifty years in 1875. The F&CJR retained a separate identity until the reorganization of the railways in 1923 when it was run by the LNER.

The attraction of the F&CJR was the tourist trade around Loch Lomond. Tours to Loch Lomond did prove popular and after the opening of the S&AR in 1882, which used a section of the F&CJR from Gartness Junction to Buchlyvie Junction, excursions to Aberfoyle added to the variety of possible excursions. Tourist excursions, however, were seasonal and the line struggled especially with strong competition from the DD&CR, eventually run by the CR. With its access into the heart of the Trossachs at Callander it meant that the F&CJR had to fight even for the tourist trade.

The western end of the route, between Drymen and Balloch proved the most successful section and by the early 1920s there were ten trains a day, some carrying pupils to the Vale of Leven Academy in Alexandria, but this was short lived. The introduction of a bus service hit the railway hard and the rail service was reduced in frequency. Sentinel steam rail cars were introduced unsuccessfully and by October 1934 passenger services were stopped although some excursions continued until the outbreak of the war in 1939. Goods services continued, however, and were even given a boost by the war, with the sparse population making the route attractive for the transport of munitions.

Soon after the nationalization of the railways in 1948 the line was severed between Gartness and Drymen, probably because the Endrick Viaduct was in a poor state. The section from Gartness Junction to Buchlyvie and onto Aberfoyle survived until November 1950. The Drymen section then became a struggling branch line and it closed in 1959 for freight as did the section between Port of Menteith and Stirling.

The F&CJR, like many other rural lines, struggled, and while it did bring pockets of prosperity, such as around Drymen Station, the line never became the hoped-for cross-country highway. The bigger railway companies always looked after their own routes first and the business scraps left could not develop or even sustain this rural line.

Exploring the Railway Heritage

The route in this section is covered by the following maps:
Explorer 347, 348, 365, 366

There were stations at Balloch, Jamestown (0.75 miles from Balloch Central), Caldarvan (3 miles), Drymen (5.75 miles), Gartness (7 miles), Balfron (9 Miles), Buchlyvie (13.25 miles), Port of Mentieth (16 miles), Kippen (20 miles), Gargunnock (23 miles) and Stirling (29 miles)

It is possible to trace the route but many sections are overgrown, bridges are missing and some sections are reclaimed by farmers. Jamestown Station has been built on and the others are private residences. The Endrick Viaduct can be crossed, now carrying a water pipeline. The only section of the trackbed which is a recognized walkway is from Drymen Station to near the site of Gartness Station. Inevitably this means that conditions underfoot can be difficult. The route taken by the railway can be followed for long distances by car using a number of roads. The exploration of the trackbed is described starting at Jamestown.

Balloch to Buchlyvie

Jamestown Station (397813) was situated to the east of the A813 as you enter Jamestown from the south. The site is occupied by Jamestown Industrial Estate and an access road covers the trackbed. From here the trackbed can be explored west across the River Leven to its junction with the railway to Balloch. The railway crossed the road by a level crossing. A footpath, with a section of original railway wall to the right leads towards the River Leven. The bridges over the River Leven and then one of its tributaries have been adapted to use as footpaths with the addition of a walkway, but some of the original piers, with cross lattice metalwork between the metal struts can still be seen. The line then veered north-west to reach the Dumbarton to Balloch line, at the Forth and Clyde Junction (391814). This direction is a bit confusing, because the original plans showed the junction facing Dumbarton. However, and apparently without parliamentary approval, the junction was

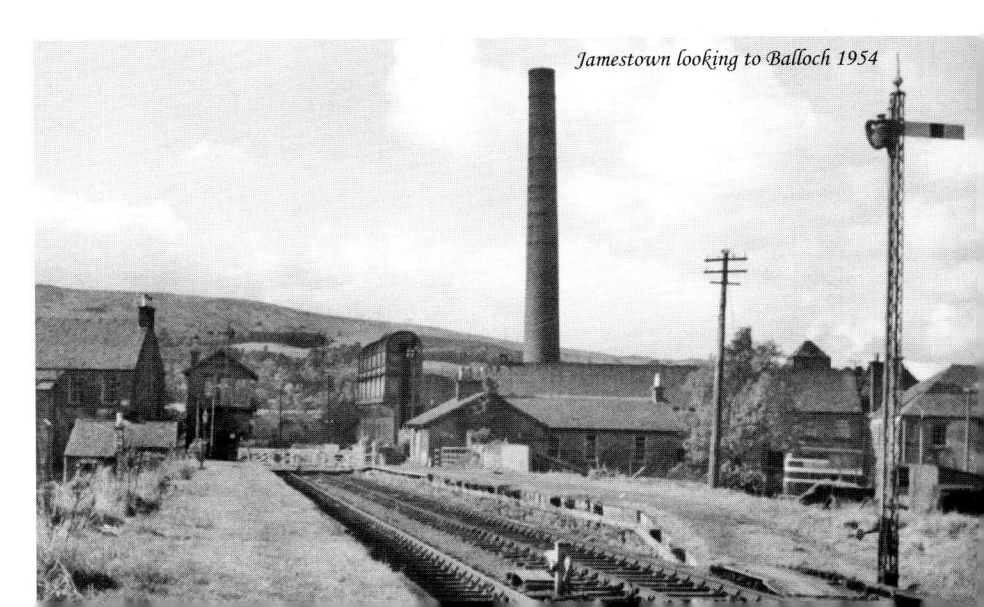

Jamestown looking to Balloch 1954

built so that the rail traffic leaving the F&CJR had to travel towards Balloch before being turned around. This awkward arrangement cannot have helped smooth running.

Exploring east from the site of Jamestown Station, an embankment carrying a siding which curved towards Dalmonach Print Works, can still be seen. The print works are now occupied by a timber merchant. The traffic generated by the siding was the major industrial input to the railway. Freight traffic generated on the rest of the line was mainly agricultural.

Beyond the former siding, buildings, part of the industrial estate block the trackbed and the next section is difficult to follow. To follow the route it is best to take the A813 south, a short distance and then turn left to follow a minor road which continues until near the site of Drymen Station. The road climbs and passes several farms. The trackbed can be seen at the bottom of the valley. To reach the trackbed take the public footpath to Dumbain Crescent found opposite the entrance to Auchencarroch Landfill Site. The trackbed is found where the railway crossed a burn. Turn east and the trackbed can be followed through a cutting to begin its journey across farmland towards Caldarvan Station. It is possible to walk along the trackbed although the route is very fragmented. Some revenue was generated by a quarry on the slopes of Blairquhomrie Moor to the south, with a tramway linking the quarry to the railway near the public footpath.

By road Caldarvan Station (439834) is reached shortly after a sharp turn to the left when the road crosses the trackbed at the site of the station. A wooden hut (a later addition) sits on the remains of the platform. Next to it is the station master's cottage. There were short sidings and their position is now

Caldarvan Station

occupied by houses. The station opened with the railway and was originally known as Kilmaronock but was renamed in 1877. Local school children caught the train from here to Alexandria for schooling. Already it is obvious that the F&CJR was a modest affair – a country route, an alternative to be used if rerouting was required. Small stations, a meandering route shaped by cost cutting, a route on the edge of the Highlands noted for its surrounding scenery and not its directness.

Beyond the station the route crosses the Gallangad Burn and then fields. Most of the trackbed has been reclaimed by the farmer. Beside the railway bridge over the burn are the abutments of another bridge. It is not clear if this was linked to the railway. Opposite Balquhain farm the railway crosses the burn again. This bridge is missing but the stumps of three timber supports and the brick abutments can be seen. In a nearby field are the rusting remains of a goods van body. Beyond the missing bridge the trackbed enters private grounds. The next section would require long detours and again it is easier to use the road, which twists and turns and crosses the trackbed several times. The Gallangad Burn eventually becomes the Catter Burn as it approaches Croftamie where it joins the River Endrick.

Near Millfaid (458855), a mile east of Drymen Station, beyond the former crossing keeper's cottage, there is a campsite. From here the trackbed can be followed, shared with a water pipeline, with the final short section into Croftamie a recognized footpath. Croftamie prospered with the railway. Originally there were only a few cottages scattered around the Catter Mill, powered by the Catter Burn but stone quarrying and a sawmill added to employment and the village grew to become Croftamie. This was the nearest point that the F&CJR got to Drymen, a distance of about two miles.

The railway crossed the A809 by a level crossing to reach Drymen Station (479864). The two storey station building overlooked a passing loop and two platforms. To the right of the line, beside the level crossing, was a signal box and behind the station buildings was a goods yard with two single and one double siding. The local laird, the Duke of Montrose, had a horse and carriage box stored in a siding for his own use. This travelled with him on his journeys. Passengers wishing to travel to Drymen could do so by using a horse and carriage operated by the grandfather of Eric Liddell, the famous Scots missionary, who won gold at the 1924 Paris Olympics, and whose life was immortalized in the 1981 film *Chariots of Fire*.

After closure the station building has been converted into a private house, still proudly proclaiming the sign 'Station House'. The yard is now an industrial estate. The trackbed has become part of the national cycle route and continues east. The water pipeline from Loch Lomond shares this part of the route. The

Drymen Station

trackbed approaches the River Endrick on a high embankment. The Endrick Viaduct, the most substantial on the route, originally consisted of a wooden structure resting on wooden trestles between masonry abutments. The viaduct was weakened by a succession of harsh winters and eventually damaged by ice flows. It lasted only sixteen years before being replaced by a stone and girder viaduct. This section of railway was the first to close and it was probably due to concerns about the state of the viaduct. Nowadays the viaduct carries the five foot diameter water pipeline across the River Endrick, on the original masonry piers, with a footpath provided on top. The trackbed then enters a railway cutting and eventually joins up with the minor road taken by the West Highland Way out of Gartness. It is better to use the road again since the trackbed is very overgrown.

Gartness to Buchlyvie Junction

As the road heads down to Gartness the railway crossed it by a level crossing to reach Gartness Station (499869). Recent development of the farm which occupies the site has left only a tiny section of the original station fencing. Gartness Junction, where the F&CJR was joined by the S&AR lies a short distance to the east and is overgrown with trees, making progress difficult. At the junction site a short detour shows the remains of the dismantled viaduct over the River Endrick. Past the junction walking is easier and continues towards the site of the missing bridge over the A81. Widening of the road has removed traces of the railway bridge but the trackbed can be seen on the east side of the road and continues, becoming a tarmac path for the last section to Balfron Station (522893). The station house, signal box and platforms have

Gartness Station looking east 1957

Gartness looking to Glasgow 1957, track of Forth & Clyde line to right

been removed along with the level crossing gates. In the background the bridge carrying the Glasgow water supply in large diameter pipes can be seen crossing the trackbed and the nearby A81. The station is now a private residence and a detour is required. The station, at two miles from Balfron, was once again not very handy for the villagers.

Balfron Station 1951

Balfron looking to Aberfoyle 1957

The trackbed runs parallel to the A81 and then crossed the A811 by a level crossing. From here to Buchlyvie Station was the highest section on the line and more earthworks were required. The route also veered north-east to reach the flat plain of the Carse of Stirling. The trackbed is very overgrown and not a recognized route. Near Gartinstarry there was another level crossing and a siding. At Buchlyvie Station (563941) the station house has become a private residence and in the gardens are the remains of platforms. A short distance beyond the station was Buchlyvie Junction where the branch to Aberfoyle continued across Flanders Moss towards Gartmore and Aberfoyle.

Buchlyvie Station 1951

Buchlyvie Junction to Stirling

The fourteen mile journey east to Stirling was undemanding for the railway engineers, with a few bridges over streams and minor earthworks to smooth out the undulating farmlands and level crossings to cross minor roads. From Buchlyvie Junction the F&CJR heads east across the flat Carse of Stirling with the Highland hills forming a constant and dramatic backdrop to the north. To the south are several ranges of hills from the Campsie Fells to the south of Buchlyvie, the Fintry Hills south of Kippen and the Gargunnock Hills south of Gargunnock. Sections of the trackbed have been reclaimed by farmers with the trackbed lost. Few of the bridges remain, though in dry weather this does not present a major obstacle. There are several railway cottages remaining beside former level crossing sites. A few level crossing gates survive, complete with warning diamonds on the gates and in one case a tree growing through the gate post. East of the M9 the trackbed disappears in a housing estate. Altogether the trackbed is not suitable for a long distance walk. The best section is from Buchlyvie Junction to Port of Menteith Station. The crossing gate at Mey's Siding (584952) remains and a lot of the trackbed is clear of obstacles but there is a missing bridge en route. Arriving at Port of Menteith Station (603960) also leaves the walker in the middle of nowhere. Port of Menteith village is four miles north of the station and Arnprior the nearest village to the south is one mile away. The station building, now a private residence still has a sign 'General Waiting Room' attached to the wall.

The route continues east but encounters two more missing bridges over streams and passes the site of Ladylands Siding (662957) where the loading bay remains. This was renamed Ladylands Platform in 1927 before closing in

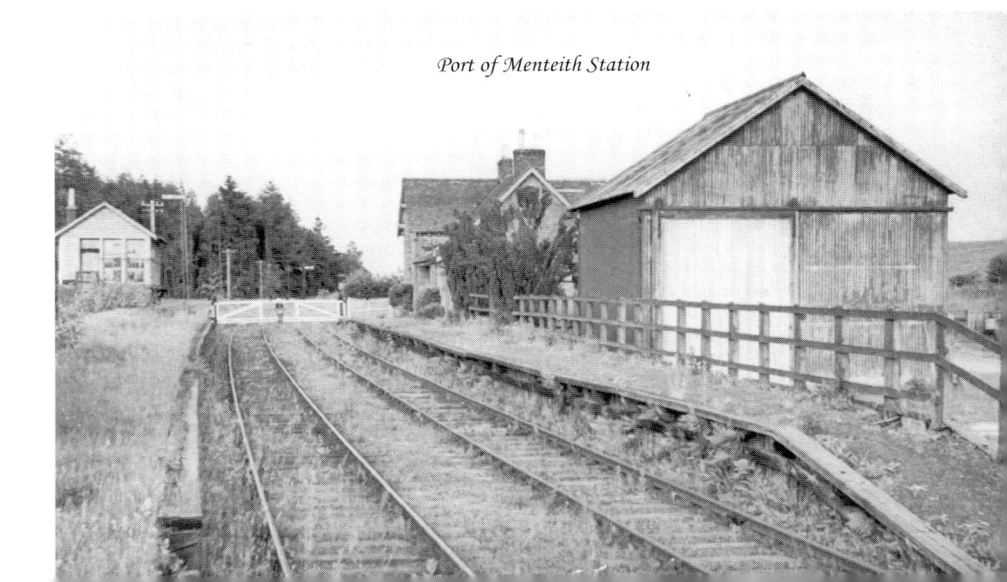

Port of Menteith Station

Sign on Port of Menteith Station building

1934. There was also briefly a siding at Fairfield a few hundred yards east of Ladylands but this has been lost to the Kippen bypass before Kippen Station is reached at the junction of the A811 with the B822.

Kippen Station (641955) was an important station with a brick signal box, a corrugated metal goods shed with overhanging canopy, station house all still intact, and a turntable which has been removed. Even part of the platform edging remains in the grounds. The station buildings are now a private residence. Kippen for many years produced grapes from the Kippen Vine, before its destruction in 1964. It was the largest vine in the world which occupied four greenhouses and was a tourist attraction. Almost 3,000 bunches of table grapes were picked in a bumper year. I wonder if any of the produce travelled by train?

Gargunnock Station (715951) was to the right of the B8075 at its junction with the A811 and is now found opposite a timber yard. Little of it remains. The timber yard is sited where the goods yard was located. The route becomes more fragmented as it approaches Stirling where the trackbed wound around the north of the castle rock to reach a junction near Stirling Station.

As it has done for many centuries, the castle perched on a rocky outcrop dominates the skyline providing a strong defensible position overlooking the surrounding countryside, a significant bulwark against invading forces. To

Kippen looking west

the south, is the battlefield of Bannockburn and to the north the Wallace Monument. This is a land rich in heroes where a nation craved its freedom. The railway provides only a modest footnote but it also had its hopes and dreams of independence and of aspirations to be great. Sadly its hope and dreams turned out to be based on a false prospectus, since the F&CJR was only a modest country route dominated by powerful neighbours, and unlike Scotland it never prospered.

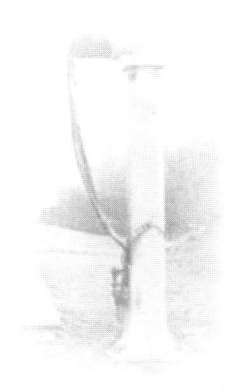

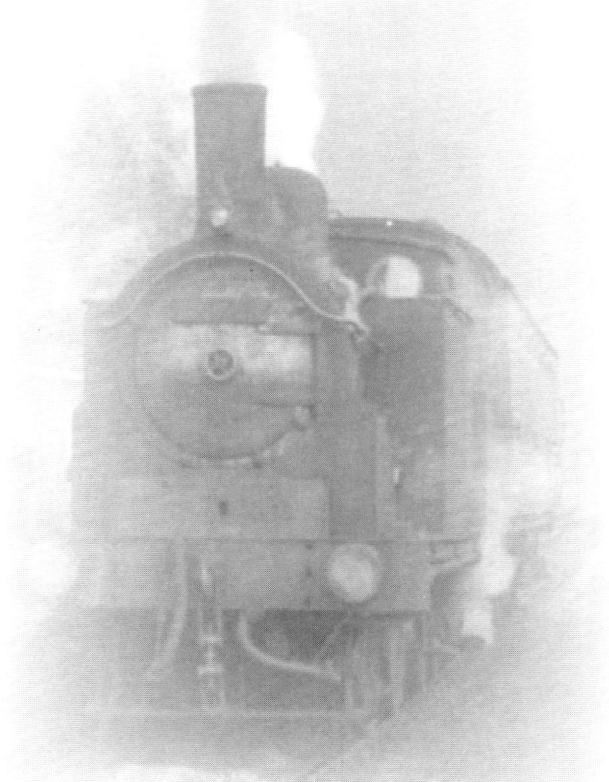

Chapter Four

The Invergarry and Fort Augustus Railway:

'Burton's Bitter Brew'

Lord Burton, a member of the famous Bass brewing dynasty, was a well-respected and rich businessman, with a reputation for looking after his workers. He also wished to contribute to the community he was part of as the owner of his large Highland estate at Glenquoich north of the Great Glen. Constructing a railway through the Great Glen, linking Fort William to Inverness, had been talked about for many years and if successful would benefit the local community and ensure easier access to his estate from the south. Like many successful businessmen he was also willing to invest and if the railway was successful he would reap the benefits, especially if it was continued to Inverness. The Invergarry and Fort Augustus Railway was created as part of a heady cocktail of the above ingredients.

Lord Burton largely funded and drove the proposals to build a railway into the Great Glen from the west. Despite the major players – the North British Railway (NBR) and the Highland Railway (HR) having signed a ten year agreement in 1889, known as the ten year truce, not to build a railway through the Great Glen, Burton was not deterred. Like the Kevin Costner film, Field of Dreams, he believed that if he built it, they would come. Kevin Costner was driven to build a baseball pitch to attract the baseball legends of an earlier generation; Lord Burton's dream was for his proposed railway not to stop at Fort Augustus but to continue to the Highland capital of Inverness. To Lord Burton this was his 'Glen of Dreams' and he believed that if he built a railway then the big railway companies would want to be involved.

It was a big gamble and ultimately spectacularly unsuccessful for many reasons – no local industry, a small population and bad timing being just a few. Also the end of the railway era, when cars were beginning to challenge the supremacy of the train was approaching and first class travellers, in particular, a good source of revenue, were about to desert the railways attracted by the new flexible form of transport offered by motor cars. Burton certainly succeeded in stirring up suspicion, intrigue and paranoia among the railway companies with an interest in the Great Glen. Paranoia was easy to create in the boardroom of companies protecting their own heartlands. After all this was a railway which aimed to shatter an uneasy truce; a branch line which left the West Highland Railway (WHR) at Spean Bridge ran through the Great Glen and ended at Fort Augustus at the southern end of Loch Ness. This branch must have appeared to the HR to be like a dagger pointing at its Inverness heartland and the HR always fiercely protected its own interests. The passing of an Act of Parliament, therefore, to construct a railway through the Glen, even if it did end thirty miles short of Inverness was unsettling and led to much manoeuvring and jockeying for position by the NBR and the HR – no one wanted to lose out.

Driven by local interest and the determined Lord Burton, the opposition was overcome and a nearly twenty five mile branch was constructed. It was built to main line standards and many wondered why. It was also constructed to be double tracked, if required. Involving the construction of several major viaducts and a tunnel, this railway passed through sparsely populated countryside with no industry and ended at a pretty but small village, Fort Augustus, more famous for its monastery. At several points it ran next to the Caledonian Canal which already provided a through route for goods, albeit slower, along the Great Glen. The railway was also at a disadvantage for goods going on to Inverness, as they had to switch to road or boat at Fort Augustus. At further expense, the railway was extended to Fort Augustus Pier which involved constructing a swing bridge over the canal, a further bridge over a river and considerable land works.

These developments must have raised further tensions in the HR boardroom – why go to this expense if you didn't intend to extend the railway to Inverness? Despite the protestations of innocence from the NBR who were willing to reaffirm the agreement signed in 1889, these were nervous moments for the HR. The threat posed by the Invergarry and Fort Augustus Railway (I&FAR) was, however, empty. No one wanted to extend the railway to Inverness. The railway simply was not viable.

When the I&FAR was finally completed in 1901 the company had run out of money and couldn't afford rolling stock. Eventually the line was opened in 1903 and operated by the HR, even though they had no direct rail link to the new railway. To ensure that they had control, the HR had paid too much for the right to operate services and soon built up large deficits. Within four years they had withdrawn. Within a week the NBR had started operations but four years later, in 1911, they ceased operations.

Lord Burton stuck to the task however, and kept supporting the project and meeting the burgeoning deficits from his own pockets until his death in 1911. In the end the NBR, by this time under the chairmanship of William Whitelaw, the former chairman of the HR, had a grudging admiration for his efforts and tenacity but also knew that they had defeated Burton's plans. The I&FAR is the story of Burton's bitter brew.

Forced with losing the route, the few locals put up a fight and after a court battle plans to scrap the line were halted. With the help of the local council, persuaded by the argument that closing the railway would mean an increased spend on the roads, the NBR were urged to start operating the route on behalf of the I&FAR again and in 1913 trains ran again. A few months later after much haggling, they bought the line and the railway owned Lovat Arms Hotel at Fort Augustus, for a fraction of the building costs. But even this was not good business, the railway was still of little value as a going concern.

The route was worked through the railway reorganisation of 1923 which created the LNER, but passenger traffic stopped at the end of 1933. In the last year there were fewer than 2000 passengers. Even the monks at the monastery, like the few locals it seems, had lost the intended habit of travelling by train. A weekly coal train, however, continued until 1946 and during the war years a logging train also ran.

This was a railway which when closed, earned more by renting out the railway premises and even by selling the grass grown on the embankments to local farmers, than it did when the line was open and trains were running. This was a line which should never have been built! In the end some of the rails were sold to Australia to be used as kangaroo proof telegraph poles. Not the outcome that Lord Burton had hoped for. His only consolation might have been the visits by King Edward, using the railway to visit Lord Burton at his estate. Rarely can royal patronage have come at such high a price.

Exploring the Railway Heritage

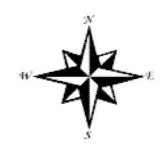

The route in this chapter are covered by the following map:
Explorer 400

There were stations at Gairlochy (2.75 miles from Spean Bridge), Invergloy Halt (7.5 miles), Invergarry (15 miles), Aberchalder (19.5 miles), Fort Augustus Town (24 miles) and Fort Augustus Pier Station (24.75 miles). The metal work of the viaducts over the River Spean, River Gloy and River Oich has been removed but the piers remain.

Several sections of this railway are worth walking but due to limited public transport care has to be taken in making plans. The section between Spean Bridge Station and the viaduct over the River Spean is very difficult to trace. On the far side of the river the trackbed can then be followed until the next missing viaduct over the River Gloy. Given the lack of buses, this section may be better walked in reverse by being dropped near the missing Gloy Viaduct and walking back to the Spean Bridge Viaduct and continuing on the north bank until you reach the village of Spean Bridge.

The section from the missing viaduct over the River Gloy until Letterfinlay Lodge Hotel is possible, but difficult to walk. From Letterfinlay, the summit of the line, until Laggan Locks the trackbed runs parallel to the road with few obstacles. From North Laggan to Aberchalder is part of the Great Glen Way and is a delightful walk along the banks of Loch Oich but tends to use General Wade's road which runs very close to the trackbed but still allows the trackbed to be explored. Beyond Aberchalder Station and Fort Augustus the trackbed is fragmented and there are obstacles. Road realignment near Fort Augustus further destroys the trackbed for some distance. An alternative would be to continue along the Great Glen Way until Fort Augustus. There are still some remnants of the railway within Fort Augustus. Given that the railway finally closed in 1946, what remains is interesting and the wonderful scenery makes any exploration that much more enjoyable.

Spean Bridge Station to the Spean Viaduct

The route started at Spean Bridge Junction (214813) half a mile west of Spean Bridge Station. A short curved part of the original I&FAR platform at the western edge of the station is all that remains of the impact on the station site today. The station on the West Highland line between Glasgow and Fort William opened in 1894 and is situated in the attractive village of Spean Bridge. The main Fort William to Inverness road, the busy A82, passes through the village crossing the River Spean before turning sharply and heading up a steep hill, past the Commando Memorial, and crossing over into the Great Glen.

Between the railway station and the realigned A82 there are no remains of the Fort Augustus branch. The junction site is now occupied by a haulage contractor with the engine shed demolished recently. On the north side of the A82 the base of a signal post can be found and the trackbed can be traced for the short distance towards the river as the ground descends into the steep sided gorge of the River Spean. This was the last section to be closed and was used as short spur for shunting, including trains until 1965. Viewing the piers of the viaduct over the River Spean, due to the foliage, is best done from the other side of the river (or in winter).

Spean Viaduct to Gloy Viaduct

There are problems at the beginning of this section. The piers of the viaduct are accessible by scrambling down the hillside from the Commando Memorial but take care! Alternatives are walking along the riverbank from Spean Bridge or retracing steps from Gairlochy. From Spean Bridge there is a path starting near the manse on the left on the road (A82) up the hill from Spean Bridge. From Gairlochy Caravan Park you walk along the trackbed to the viaduct site and then retrace your steps. Conditions underfoot are difficult but there are good views of the spectacular gorge. Retaining walls abound in the confines of the gorge. The tall concrete piers reach seventy-six feet above the river and the four metal sections were supported by five concrete piers. Whichever route is chosen, take care as conditions underfoot are usually very muddy.

The Commando memorial with its views towards the Nevis mountain range is a fitting tribute to the dedication of the men who trained so hard in this area and inflicted a new and fierce style of warfare. Their training base at Achnacarry House, on the north side of Loch Lochy, meant that the commandos must have been familiar with this railway. My uncle, James Wham, who was a sergeant in the commandos, received the Military Medal at Anzio. His further exploits provided inspiration for the film *The Guns of Navarone*. Sadly additions to the memorial remembrance garden are still being added due to recent conflicts. Our respect and gratitude is owed to them all.

Gairlochy Caravan Park now fills the space occupied by Gairlochy Station (188835). The tarmac path through the park follows the route of the railway line. Looking from the entrance (towards Spean Bridge) there is a concrete

Gairlochy 1950

abutment to the left which formed part of an elaborate footbridge over the line. The footbridge was connected to a large 170 yard long island platform on which was situated the main station building constructed with a wood and stone base with a projecting awning all round. The signal cabin was situated on the platform. Partitions at each end of the building provided relief from the wind. The platform and buildings have been demolished and replaced with a house. A loading bank remains and between it and the new building, campers sleep on what were the three goods sidings. The LNER converted both Gairlochy and Invergarry stations into holiday accommodation in an attempt to generate revenue.

Beyond the caravan park the railway crossed the B8004. There has been road realignment here to allow better access to the caravan park. The single metal plate bridge does still exist adorned with unfriendly warnings about fly-tipping and fishing and protected with barbed wire. Given that railway walkers are not interested in either, access to the trackbed can be made further on.

The trackbed now swings round to offer views of Gairlochy and its canal locks where the Caledonian Canal reaches Loch Lochy, the first of several lochs it uses to reach Inverness. The canal built by the famous Scottish engineer Thomas Telford was the most northerly canal in Britain and was opened in 1822. It extends for sixty miles, of which only 22 miles are man made and the rest uses the many natural lochs found in the Great Glen. Nowadays most traffic on the canal system consists of leisure craft. The isolated trackbed provides a wonderful and changing viewpoint of the spectacular scenery from the hillside above Loch Lochy as the route snakes through several woodlands towards the A82 near Glenfintaig.

Gloy Viaduct to Invergarry Station

The route passed under the A82 to reach another steep side gorge. Not as wide as Spean Gorge, it still required a substantial viaduct to cross the river which runs through Glen Gloy. Again only the four concrete abutments remain which are difficult to see given that the steep sides of the gorge are very overgrown with trees. The end spans were each of fifty feet with the central span one hundred feet.

A minor road allows the gorge to be crossed and a scramble allows the trackbed to be regained but it's dangerous and slippery and the next section, towards Invergloy Halt, can be overgrown. My advice would be to miss it out. Indeed I took one of the few buses to near Glenfintaig Farm and walked back to Spean Bridge.

The site of Invergloy Halt (230885) was in front of what is now 'The Heathers Bed and Breakfast Guest House'. The halt, which had a simple wooden shelter at the far end of the single platform, was located on what is now the lawn in front of the new house. A wooden signal post, a recent addition, makes the connection obvious. The house is found beside the A82 nearly opposite Invergloy House which the halt was built to serve. Passengers had to request that the train stopped at the halt. A single metal plate railway bridge is found just before the site of the halt.

From Invergloy Halt the next section on the steep eastern slopes of Loch Lochy provides dramatic views across the loch and of the many small boats, traversing the water system. The railway's construction required numerous small bridges to cross the many streams flowing down the hillside and opposite

Bridge at Invergloy, Fort Augustus Branch 1971

Letterfinlay Lodge Hotel, high on the hillside, there is an impressive three arch concrete viaduct fording a stream. Further along there is a metal footbridge over the line. The summit of the line is near here and there was also a signal box designed to control a 361 yard passing loop intended to be used to break the long section from Gairlochy to Invergarry, a distance of almost thirteen miles. This was never used and was abandoned before the line opened. The location of the signal box is not clear and erosion has also reduced the width of the track. From here the trackbed can be followed to Laggan, the last section through a forest which restricts views. As the trackbed drops in height it passes to the rear of the Corriegour Lodge Hotel where a private siding was opened to load timber.

The Caledonian Canal links Loch Lochy, which ends at Laggan, with Loch Oich. At the western end are the Laggan Locks and at the other end of this short section of the canal is the Laggan Swing Bridge. The railway trackbed continues to the west of the canal and the A82, at the edge of the forest.

Invergarry Station to Fort Augustus

Behind the Great Glen Water Park, the trackbed becomes a section of the Great Glen Way, a seventy-three mile long distance footpath from Fort William to Inverness. The path uses parts of the railway trackbed and General Wade's road and this arrangement continues, for the next 4 miles, until near Aberchalder Swing Bridge. General Wade's road was built, around 1727, to link the military garrisons at Fort William, Fort Augustus and Fort George on the Moray Firth.

Behind the Great Glen Water Park complex is the site of Invergarry Station (305984). On the banks of the loch, although the site is now so overgrown that this is not obvious, was the station for Invergarry – on the wrong side of the loch and some three miles from the village. The station was very isolated. The station buildings were situated on a large island platform which was accessed by a subway protected by a covered ramp. The station building, bigger than Gairlochy—there were three chimney stacks instead of two—had an awning extending on all sides. On the loch side this was unusually extended over the track with a vee-shaped ridge over the line. A single siding with loading bank and goods shed was sited to the loch side of the platform. There was a private waiting room for use by the laird of Glengarry, who lived at Glengarry House on the west bank of the loch. King Edward visited at least twice enroute to Lord Burton's Glenquoich Lodge. This was a great honour in Edwardian times and showed the elevated social circle in which Lord Burton moved. At least once, the King travelled on to Fort Augustus.

Invergarry looking north - 1914

Today the station is found beside a forestry track. The site is very overgrown but the large platform can be discerned as can the subway, the height of which is surprisingly low. Maybe the King was very short! In its final years, thousands of tons of timber were loaded onto the railway at Invergarry Station.

Beyond the station site the Great Glen Way does deviate from the trackbed for a short distance but both path and trackbed soon resume their journey beside the loch through mixed woodland. The journey is both peaceful and beautiful in an enchanting location. Across the loch the ruins of Invergarry Castle and later the village of Invergarry can be seen. On the other side of

Invergarry 1931

Loch Oich tunnel

the loch, where the River Garry flows into Loch Oich, is the village of Invergarry and an important road junction where the road to Kyle of Lochalsh and the Skye Bridge (A87) branches.

There are many remnants of the railway in this section including several elaborate concrete castellated bridges and long sections of concrete retaining walls and the remains of linesman's huts. Near a shoreside cottage at Leitirfearn is another viaduct. A sixty-seven yard long tunnel was also required, cut through solid rock, complete with mock castellated entrance. Its construction helped to shield the railway, which would have had to be extended onto the loch, from the gaze of those in the big house opposite. The tunnel and the cutting on the approach to it are waterlogged and the tunnel cannot be accessed. The tunnel is best viewed from the General's road, where the crumbling façade on the east side can be viewed. Two rusted metal troughs, supported by brick piers, still carry water across the trackbed to the loch side. This next section was very vulnerable to landslides and the troughs helped to carry away excess water.

Loch Oich side, water drainage channel over the trackbed

As the trackbed emerges from the woodland, it crosses the Calder Burn by a low plate girder bridge supported on five sets of circular piers. The viaduct has been renovated. The Great Glen Way then veers to the left following the loch side to Aberchalder Swing Bridge where it crosses to the opposite side of the canal and continues towards Fort Augustus. This is an attractive and easier walk to Fort Augustus.

The railway trackbed crosses farmland towards the A82 where it once bridged the road. The rail bridge has been removed. The trackbed continues on an embankment until the site of Aberchalder Station (345041) located beside a road bridge carrying a minor road. The station site is to the west of the road bridge and consisted of a single platform with a short siding on a gradient of one in sixty-six. The remains of the concrete platform can still be seen although the trackbed has been largely filled in. The station building was

Aberchalder looking south 1937

similar to Gairlochy but with the awning only on one side. The building was destroyed in a fire in the 1950s. It had been used by a fruit merchant for a few years previously.

The trackbed continues for another four miles and for the first half of the journey through a forest. There are gaps and it can be difficult to follow. Beyond the forest it skirts to the right of Loch Uanagan and then is lost to road realignment until the outskirts of Fort Augustus.

Fort Augustus

The station site in Fort Augustus (375097) is now part of the campus of Kilchuimen Academy. Kilchuimen being an earlier name for Fort Augustus before the fort was built. The station had an island platform and a single platform. The station building at right angles to the track was long and had four sets of chimneys. The single platform was to the right as you looked towards the canal. The single platform and the platform opposite were for trains terminating at the station. The through platform was to the left, on the west side of the island platform. Part of it still exists, shoring up the school's car park with the end ramp protruding through the fence onto the pavement of the road beside the canal. To the right of the single platform was an engine shed, goods shed and turntable.

The railway continued, by a swing bridge, to cross the Caledonian Canal at the top of a sequence of five locks which took the canal down to the level of Loch Ness. Canal users complained about the time taken for the swing bridge to be used to allow a train to cross. They needn't have bothered, given the few times it was used.

The railway then crossed the River Oich. The three piers and the abutments of this bridge over the River Oich remain, complete with castellated tops and inset crosses, presumably to suggest a link with the local monastery. The ornate piers still attract attention today from visitors, who are probably puzzled, until they realise what they are.

Fort Augustus Station under construction 1903

This turned out to be 'a bridge too far', with the final section along with the first part from Spean Bridge Station to the crossing over the River Spean absorbing a disproportionate amount of the total construction costs. The trackbed then crossed over the A82 before swinging round to the pier at Fort Augustus Pier Station (385099). This last stretch required extensive cutting of a rock face. At the end of the line was a simple station building with one chimney and with a station sign which simply read 'Pier'. There was a turning loop. The station was open for the summer seasons only between 1903 and 1906 but it continued to be open for freight until 1938. No sign remains of the station today which now lies in private ground. The remnants of the pier can still be seen.

From here the view was towards Inverness. Having crossed the River Oich the railway was poised to continue towards the Highland capital on the west side of Loch Ness. The call to extend the line never came and the wildly ambitious gamble died in this remote Highland village. Today even the monks have gone, and sightings of the Loch Ness Monster are about as credible as sightings of a train. It was a brave attempt by Lord Burton but the times were wrong and the railway era was ending. His 'Glen of Dreams' had become a nightmare.

Fort Augustus railway pier and Loch Ness

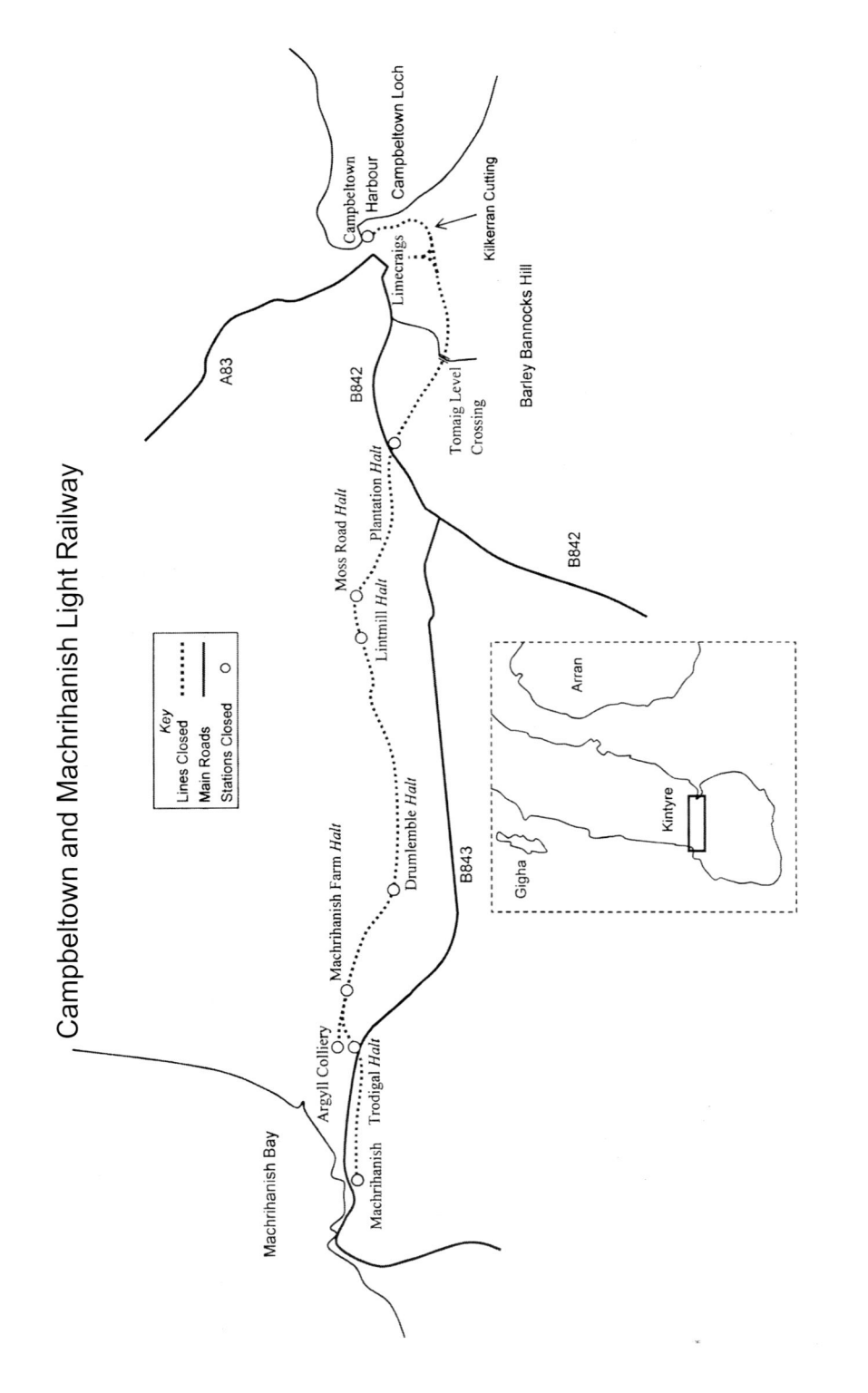

Campbeltown and Machrihanish Light Railway

Chapter Five

The Campbeltown and Machrihanish Light Railway:

'Coal, Whisky and Tom Morris'

The Campbeltown and Machrihanish Light Railway was one of Scotland's most remote railways near the southern end of the Kintyre peninsula on Scotland's west coast. The nearest railway is twenty five miles away in Northern Ireland and the nearest Scottish railway station is at Oban almost ninety miles north. The peninsula is linked to the Argyll coastline by a narrow mile wide isthmus at its northern end, at Tarbert and Kintyre is often called the 'mainland island'. Campbeltown, the only town in Kintyre, is nearer the southern end of the peninsula at the end of a long road from Glasgow which winds down the western coast of Kintyre before the road turns east to cross the low-lying area known as the 'Laggan', to reach Campbeltown on the east coast situated around Campbeltown Loch. When the railway opened, helped by the Light Railway Act, and its easing of restrictions, the Kintyre peninsula was easier to reach by boat from Glasgow than by road. Indeed the first car was only seen in the town in 1898, a few years before the railway opened to passengers in 1906. However remote Campbeltown was to most people, it was famous for one thing – it was the whisky capital of the world. In the town, at the turn of the nineteenth century, were sited in excess of thirty distilleries with puffers ready to take the whisky barrels to Glasgow for blending from the harbour at Campbeltown Loch.

The line had opened in 1877, to serve the coal mines near the village of Drumlembie just over four miles west of Campbeltown and when they were worked out, the railway was extended further west, to service the Argyll coal mine close to Machrihanish. The coal had been mined since the fifteenth century and was the source of heating for many castles. The coal field was an extension of the Ayrshire coalfield, emerging from under the Firth of Clyde, but the coal was not of great quality and only suitable for power stations and distilleries. A lot of the coal was exported to Northern Ireland. Campbeltown has a sheltered harbour and was the only site suitable for exporting coal from the Argyll coalfield. At Machrihanish Bay there were sand dunes only and no harbour, so the coal had to be transported six miles across the 'Laggan' to reach Campbeltown. Early attempts to open a canal, and the land was certainly flat enough, were unsuccessful. While many believed that the railway was built on the route of the canal, in fact they only shared a common course for a few hundred yards.

When the Speyside region in the north-east of Scotland started to compete for the whisky market in Glasgow, they provided unpeated smoother whiskies increasingly popular with blenders. Campbeltown's whisky style was originally peated but they quickly changed and used coal from the Argyll coal field for distilling, much to the relief of the townsfolk who lived with the smell of burning peat belching from over thirty distillery chimneys around the confined harbour site. Distilleries on the neighbouring islands of Islay and Jura, visible off Kintyre's west coast also used coal from Kintyre.

In May 1904 with local interests working together — the coal mine owners, the distilleries and the steamer owners — the Argyll Railway Company was formed. The mineral line from the coal depot in Campbeltown, where it originally stopped, was extended down to the harbour, and on the eastern side of the peninsula the railway was extended from the Argyll colliery to behind the Ugadale Arms Hotel in Machrihanish. Just over two years later in August 1906 the railway was opened to passengers and within three weeks over ten thousand passengers had travelled on the route.

Part of the attraction was Machrihanish—marketed for the tourists as a seaside resort. Day visitors could sail 'doon the watter' from Glasgow, past the Island of Arran, on the new faster turbine steamers introduced at the beginning of the twentieth century, to reach Campbeltown where they could join the train to cross Kintyre. With its famous golf links visitors could have a round of golf on one of the world's best courses, before returning in the evening to Glasgow. Many golf experts claim that Machrihanish Golf Course has the finest opening hole in the world, designed by Tom Morris, an early Scottish winner of the British Open Golf Championship. The remoteness of the golf course and its associations with Tom Morris added to the course's allure.

The line was single track with a narrow gauge, two-foot-three-inches; after all it could suit itself, with no possible connections to other railway networks. Engineering works were minimal with the highest embankment required, on the flat land between Campbeltown and Machrihanish, being only six feet and the deepest cutting only twenty-eight feet, although gradients on the steep climb from Campbeltown, at one in thirty-three, were demanding. There was only one overbridge on the railway network at Limecraigs. None of the

Hall Street, Campbeltown showing the minimal construction work required

stations had platforms, in Campbeltown the railway stopped on the quayside and at Machrihanish in a field. There were halts at Plantation, Moss Road, Lintmill, Drumlembie, Machrihanish Farm, Trodigal and Machrihanish. Only Machrihanish had a modest station building, although Drumlembie had a shelter, which was sadly often unfit for purpose, being subject to vandalism.

There were three trains on weekdays and three extra on a Saturday. The train stopped by request at halts. An express which ran without stopping between the two termini, operated during the summer months but it took the same length of time. Adverts suggested the journey took only twenty minutes —thirty minutes was more typical. There were some unusual obstacles. Near the Campbeltown end at Barley Bannocks Hill was a rifle range, with riflemen firing at right angles across the line.

The railway closed in 1931, two years after the pits closed and after a losing battle with two bus companies, who waged a bitter war for passengers and took the local passenger traffic, such as it was, away from the railway. Excursion traffic was the only remaining business and it was no longer sufficient. The Campbeltown and Machrihanish Light Railway had lasted twenty five years.

The whisky production in the town had also experienced a drastic decline, with the impact of prohibition in America and problems with quality. The distilleries became too complacent believing that there would always be a market in Glasgow, but with recession this was no longer true and cost cutting impacted on quality. Ironically, railways played a part in this with the lines north of Perth capable of delivering Speyside whisky to the blenders, in the central belt of Scotland, overnight.

The railway went into liquidation in 1933. The colliery reopened in 1946, with 100,000 tons per week being produced at peak in 1957 but poor conditions underground and a shrinking market led to its final closure in 1967. When the coal mine was reopened, all coal was removed by road as by this time everything in the railway had been scrapped.

The Kintyre peninsula was used for a different type of transport, during the cold war. Machrihanish Airfield, now largely mothballed, was developed as a major staging post for the Americans to transport troops and materials across the Atlantic, if circumstances demanded. With, at one time, the longest landing strip in Europe, the airfield would have been a major hub of activity in event of a war. There were also rumours of classified airplanes, such as stealth fighters, using the airfield for test flights.

Having closed so long ago, and with modest engineering required, little remains of the railway today. It is still worthwhile visiting Kintyre, because of its remoteness and beauty. The Mull of Kintyre, the hilly southern tip of the Kintyre peninsula with its views across the narrow channel to Ireland, made famous by Paul McCartney's song of the same name, the still famous golf links and the rugged coastline and Celtic history all make the trip worthwhile. Even the whisky distilleries are experiencing a new lease of life.

Campbeltown's architectural heritage is still influenced by the lost distilleries; a few of them can still be seen, often with only their frontage remaining. Campbeltown is sometimes described as 'Glasgow by the sea' because tenements line many of the streets and later buildings, often on the sites of demolished distilleries, still imitate this style. The views over Campbeltown Loch towards Davaar Island provide a welcome contrast.

Exploring the Railway Heritage

The route is covered by the following map: Explorer 356.

There was a station at Campbeltown and also at Machrihanish, (6 miles from Campbeltown). In between there were halts at Plantation (1.75 miles from Campbeltown), Moss Road (2.5 miles), Lintmill (2.7 miles), Drumlembie (4.5 miles), Machrihanish Farm Halt (5.4 miles) and Trodigal (5.6 miles). Sadly very little is left. The location of the two station sites can be identified but nothing remains.

The railway could not have got closer to its main passenger source – the engine and carriages were next to the quay at Campbeltown harbour (721204) ready to receive passengers disembarking at the Old Quay. The rails stopped at the edge of what was the Christian Institute on Hall Street, now council offices, short of what is now a roundabout. There were no platforms and the railway offices were on the ground floor of the tenement block next to the picture house, a few hundred yards east. The picture house, incidentally, is one of the oldest surviving picture houses in Scotland; it was opened in 1923, and is still showing films. Hall Street is now a dual carriageway and rumour has it, that the rails are buried underneath the palm trees of the central reservation. Many believe that sections of the rails also remain buried under farmers' fields or near the mine heads.

Hall Street, Campbeltown - the picture house was constructed in the gap between the buildings

Hall Street, Campbeltown today

    The New Quay which lies to the east of the Old Quay was not actually new, and at over a hundred years old, was more of a breakwater. Until recently it was only in use during wartime or for loading coal onto cargo ships. A siding extended to the end of the New Quay where a steam crane was located. There was a recent attempt to start a ferry service to Ballycastle in Northern Ireland, which has led to the development of the New Quay with road improvements allowing better access. Wood is now loaded onto ships at the New Quay and wind turbine sections are landed on it to be transported to the expanding wind farms on the peninsula. The railway once extended across Quarry Green, now a park, and crossed Kilkerran Road (723200). The Quarry Green area was reclaimed from the sea when the railway was built. The route then entered the only deep cutting on the line, now a footpath and community woodlands, and climbed at a gradient of one in thirty-three. At the entrance to the cutting is a memorial to George Armour of Chicago, a one-time resident of Campbeltown who made his fortune in America from the beef business.

    Nowadays the trackbed emerges from the cutting into a landscaped area with playing fields. The scene has been totally transformed. This area was, and still is, known as Limecraigs – the cutting ends on Limecraigs Road, which is built over the trackbed. It was where the railway had its workshops and engine and carriage sheds. They were mainly to the right of the trackbed and in a triangular junction with the original railway terminus which was to the right and extended to the west side of the Gaelic Church. The original terminus of the railway, before it was extended to the quayside, was beside the Gaelic Church with coal being carted by barrow from the coal ree to the quayside, an unnecessary double handling. Across the coal ree was the only overbridge on the line which connected the Kintyre Nurseries, which had been divided when the line was laid. Campbeltown Hospital now covers most of the area and nothing remains to connect the scene to the railway age.

At the eastern edge of the triangular junction was an unusual hazard – a rifle range. Already in place when the railway was opened, the rifle range was still being used and a red flag raised when shots were to be fired. There are no reports of trains been shot at, so the safety arrangements must have been effective. The rifle range extended up the steep slope of Barley Bannocks Hill, at right angles to the railway. The trackbed continued west towards Tomaig Road. The section between the Limecraigs Road and Tomaig Road was known as the Tomaig Bank, a steep climb for the trains and in the other direction a steep drop towards the quayside or the coal ree.

A housing estate has been built over this section, but not all is lost, because to the west of the Tomaig Road (721198), at what was a level crossing is a short section of trackbed. Its narrowness reminds you of the narrow gauge nature of the railway, and its continued existence is due to an underground oil pipe from the NATO facility on Campbeltown Loch to Machrihanish Airfield. Eventually the trackbed becomes only a raised edge to a field before petering out as it approached the section known as Plantation, where the railway once again crossed the road just after the farm road to North Moy. At one time next to the level crossing was a public house, which because it served no oatcakes with its whisky was immortalised as the 'hungry hoose'. There was a halt at North Moy. A new house is built over the north side where the trackbed

Tomaig Road level crossing

cut across the road at an acute angle. Beyond the house the narrow trackbed returns for a few hundred yards, with the pipeline still buried underneath. Farming has removed most visible signs of the railway for the rest of the route. However on Aros Road (which leads to Campbeltown Airport) there are two gates almost opposite one another. Heading west from the road, the Chiscan Water is reached. The concrete abutments of the rail bridge (688206) remain but the wooden planks placed over the I-beam girders have been removed. This was close to the site of Lintmill passing loop and what could be described as a miniature signal box. The concrete abutments are the last remnant of the railway until close to the Argyll Colliery, on the outskirts of Machrihanish. There is no sign of the halt at Drumlembie.

To the east of the access road to West Machrihanish Farm the trackbed divided with the original track keeping to the southern bank of the Machrihanish Water and the light railway line cutting south-west to cross the B843 on the approaches to Machrihanish. Beside the entrance to the Machrihanish Caravan and Camping site is a building associated with the colliery.

The trackbed then ran behind the houses to the south of the road passing behind the Ugadale Arms Hotel. A long stone wall links the scene with the past. New housing has again removed most signs of the railway. The railway ran several yards from the wall. Where the stone wall changes direction there is a new house situated on the site of the original modest station building at Machrihanish (634206), which was wooden with a corrugated roof which slightly overhung the front. The station was behind the old mission hall. The end of the line was just to the left of the road.

Train behind the Ugadale Hotel (now Kintyre Hotel and Cottages), near Machrihanish Station

The views towards Islay and Jura are stunning, but the exposure to winds sweeping in from the Atlantic is also obvious. To the west was the site of the first wireless transmission across the Atlantic and the tall transmitter masts can be seen in the background of some early photographs. The route which started at the Christian Institute in Hall Street and ended behind the Mission Hall in Machrihanish was not worth saving. The decline of coal and the seasonal nature of the tourist trade hurried its departure. For the railway, however, memories are all that remains, sometimes buried deep, if you listen to the locals.

Further Reading

In preparing the manuscript the author consulted the following books:

Gordon Biddle & O.S. Nock, *Railway Heritage of Britain,* Studio Editions, 1990

R.V. J. Butt, *Directory of Railway Stations,* Patrick Stephens Ltd, 1995

Bernard Byrom, *Railways of Upper Strathearn,* Oakwood Press, 2004

M.H. Ellison, *Scottish Railway Walks,* Cicerone Press Guide, 1989

A.D. Farr, *Campbeltown and Machrihanish Light Railway,* Oakwood Press, 1987

C. J. Gammell, *Scottish Branch Lines,* Oxford Publishing Co. 1999

Nigel S.C. MacMillan, *Campbeltown and Machrihanish Light Railway,* Plateway Press, 1993

John McGregor, *West Highland Railway,* John Donald ,2005

John Mitchell, *Rise and Decline of the Railway in Drymen and District,* Drymen and District Local History Society, 2003

Gavin Morrison, *Scottish Railways - Then & Now,* Ian Allan Publishing, 1999

Keith Sanders and Douglas Hodgins, *British Railways, Past and Present, North West Scotland,* 1998

John Thomas, *Forgotten Railways Scotland,* David & Charles, 1976

John Thomas, *Regional History of the Railways of Great Britain, Scotland: The Lowlands and the Borders.* David & Charles, 1984

John Thomas, *West Highland Railway,* David St John Thomas, 1984

John Thomas, *Callander and Oban Railway,* David St John Thomas Publisher, 1991

John Thomas and David Turnock, *Regional History of the Railways of Great Britain Volume 15 North of Scotland,* David St John Thomas Publisher, 1989

Nigel Welbourn, *Lost Lines, Scotland,* Ian Allan Publishing, 1994

Useful Contacts and Websites

Caledonian Railway Association: www.crassoc.org.uk

Railscot, A History of Britain's Railways Railway Website: www.railbrit.co.uk

North British Railway Study Group: www.noble101.freeserve.co.uk

Railway Ramblers: www.railwayramblers.org.uk

Scottish Railway Preservation Society: Bo'ness Station, Union Street, West Lothian, EH51 9AQ; www.srps.org.uk

Sustrans: Scottish Office, 162 Fountainbridge, Edinburgh EH3 9RX; www.sustrans.org.uk

Jim Caution's memoirs of Craig-Nan-Cailleach, Loch Lubnaig: www.btinternet.com/~cheekycaution/jim1.htm

Historic Scotland: www.historic-scotland.gov.uk/

Scotland the Movie Location Guide: www.scotlandthemovie.com

INDEX

Plates shown in bold

A

Aberchalder 106
Aberchalder Station 106, 113, **113**
Aberchalder Swing Bridge 110, 113
Aberdeen 13, 14, 41
Aberfoyle 8, 71-73, 79-81, 84, 85, 87, **87**, 88, 91, 92, 98
Aberfoyle Station 87, 88
Achmore Woods 54
Achnacarry House 107
Achraw Hill 44
Alexandria 92, 95
Allt an Fhionn 45
Allt Coire Chaorach Burn 35
Allt na-h-Atha 45
Anderson's Piano 15
Appin 57, 58, 60, 65, 66
Appin Station 64, 65
Ardchyle Viaduct 33, 53
Ardgour 66
Ardmucknish Bay 62
Ardoch Burn 19, 20
Ardrishaig 17
Argyll Colliery 124
Arnprior 99
Arrochar 17, 36
Auchenteck Farm 19
Auchentroig Burn 84
Auchessan Farm 35
Auchindarroch Caravan Park 66

B

Back O'Loch Halt 73
Balfron Station 90, 96, **97**, **98**
Balglass Farm 77
Ballachulish 9, 15, 16, 57-60, 67, 68
Ballachulish Bridge 67
Ballachulish Ferry 60, 67, **69**

Ballachulish Ferry Station 67
Ballachulish Pier 66
Ballachulish Station 67, **68**
Balloch 89, 90, 92-94
Balloch, Jamestown 92
Balloch Central 92
Ballycastle 122
Balquhain Farm 95
Balquhidder 9, 16, 18, 23, 26-28, 39, 41, 44, 49
Balquhidder Braes Caravan Park 28, 43
Balquhidder Glen 16, 26, 28, 33, 53
Balquhidder Junction 40-42
Balquhidder Station 26, **26**, 27-29
Balquhidder Station underpass **42, 43**
Banavie 58
Bannockburn 101
Barcaldine 63
Barcaldine Halt **63**
Barley Bannocks Hill 119, 123
Beech Tree Inn 82
Ben Cruachan 17, 37
Benderloch 58, 60, 62, 63
Benderloch Station 66
Ben Lawers 51, 54, 56
Ben Ledi 21, 23
Ben More 32, 35, 53
Benmore Farm 35
Ben Vorlich 24, 28, 44, 45
Blanefield 72, 73, 80
Blanefield Print Works 79
Blanefield Station 79, **79**, 81
Blane Valley 77
Blane Water 79, 80
'Blondin' 68
Bochastle Hill 23
Bowling 89, 90, 91
Bracklinn Falls 21, 22
Braes of Balquhidder. 53
Bridge of Keltie 20
Broomhill Hospital 74
Buchlyvie 72, 73, 85, 90, 92, 93, 99
Buchlyvie Junction 83, 84, 91, 98, 99
Buchlyvie Junction double bridge **84**
Buchlyvie Station 84, 98, **98**

C

Caldarvan Station 94, **94**
Calder Burn 112
Caledonian Canal 104, 108, 110, 114
Callander 9, 14-16, 18, 21, **22**, 23, 24, 37, 39, 53, 91
Callander Station 21, **21**, 23
Callander ticket platform **21**
Campbeltown 117-122
Campbeltown Airport 124
Campbeltown Hospital 123
Campbeltown Loch 117, 120, 123
Campsie Alum Works 76
Campsie Fells 8, 71, 75, 77, 78, 80, 88, 99
Campsie Glen 73
Campsie Glen Station 78
Campsie Junction 73
Carse of Stirling 8, 84, 90, 98, 99
Castle Stalker 65
Catter Burn 95
Catter Mill 95
'Chariots of Fire' 95
Charles Macintosh 77
Chiscan Water 124
Commando Memorial 107
Comrie 29, 39-42, 48, 49, 52
Connel Airfield 62
Connel Ferry Bridge **60**, 61, **61**, 62
Connel Ferry Station 58, 60, 62
Corriegour Lodge Hotel 110
Craig-nan-Cailleach 24, **24**
Craigendoran 36
Craigmore 88
Creagan 60
Creagan Bridge 63, **64**
Creagan Farm 64
Creagan Station 63-65, **65**
Crianlarich 7, 9, 14, 17, 18, 32, 35-37, 39, 53, 72
Crianlarich Junction 18, 37
Crianlarich Lower 35, 37
Crianlarich Upper Station 37
Crieff 9, 39, 40, 41, 52
Crieff Junction 41
Croftamie 95
Cultybraggan Camp 49

D

Dalchonzie Halt 48, **48**
Dalginross 49
Dalmally 14
Dalmonach Print works 94
Dalveich Farm 42, 44
Davaar Island 120
David Marshall Lodge 88
Dochart Viaduct 56
Doon Hill 87
Doune 18-20, 22
Doune Castle 20
Doune Ponds 19
Doune Station **20**
'Dr Finlay's Casebook' 22
Drumfechan (Gartmore) 85, **86**
Drumlembie 117, 119, 121, 124
Drummond Trout Farm and Fishery 49
Drumvaich 20
Drymen Station 90, 92-95, **96**
Duke's Pass 88
Dumgoyach Hill 73, 80
Dumgoyne 73, 77, 80, 82
Dumgoyne Station 81, **81**
Dunblane 8, 9, 13, 18, 19, 22
Dundee 41
Dundurn Viaduct 48
Dundurn Wood 48
Dunglass Hill 78
Duntreath Castle 80
Duror 60, 66
Duror Station 66

E

Earthquake House 49
Edinburgh 8, 18
Edinchip Farm 29
Edinchip Viaduct 27, 43
Eilean Balnagowan 66
Endrick Viaduct 92, 93, 95
Endrick Water 82
'Eye of the Needle' 62

F

Falkirk 14
Falls of Dochart 52, 55
Falls of Leny 23, 24, 37
Falls of Lora 59, 61
Fillan Viaduct 37
Fin Glen 78
Fin Glen Burn 78
Finlarig Castle 56
Finlarig Power Station 57
Flanders Moss 84, 85, 98
Fort Augustus 103-107, 110, 113, 114
Fort Augustus Pier 104, 106, 115, **115**
Fort Augustus Pier Station 106, 115
Fort Augustus Station under construction **114**
Fort George 110
Forth Valley 71, 87, 88
Fort William 7, 9, 36, 37, 57, 58, 67, 72, 80, 103, 107, 110

G

Gairlochy 106-108, 110, 113
Gairlochy Caravan Park 107
Gairlochy Station 107, **108**
Gallangad Burn 95
Gareloch 22
Gargunnock Station 100
Gartmore 73, 86, **86**, 87, 98
Gartmore House 86
Gartmore Station 85
Gartness 73, 80, 82, 83, 90, 92, 96, **97**
Gartness Junction 72, 82, 83, 91, 92, 96
Gartrenich Bridge 85, **85**
Gateway to the Trossachs 71
General Wade's road 106, 110
'Geordie' 85
George Armour 122
Glasgow 8, 22, 35, 36, 41, 71-73, 79, 80, 82, 89-91, 107, 117, 118,
Glazert Water 74-78
Glen Beich 44
Glenbruar Viaduct 37
Glen Coe 58, 68
Glen Dochart 14, 17, 26, 33, 51, 53, 54

Glen Dochart Caravan Park 34
Glen Dochart Viaduct 53
Gleneagles 41
Glen Falloch 14, 35-37, 72
Glenfinnan Viaduct. 7
Glenfintaig 108
Glenfintaig Farm 109
Glengarry House 110
Glen Gloy 109
Glengoyne 80, 81, 82
Glengoyne Distillery 80
Glen Lednock 41
'Glen of Dreams' 103, 105
Glen Ogle 9, 14, 16, 18, 27, 30, 32, 33, 37, 51, 52, 54
Glenogle Farm 30
Glenoglehead 15-18, 27, 29, 30, 32, 37, 50, 53, 54
Glenoglehead Crossing 18, 32, 33
Glenoglehead Station 53
Glen Ogle Viaduct **29**, 31
Glenquoich 103, 110
Glensanda Quarry 66
Glentarken 45
Glentarken Viaduct abutments **46**
Glentarken Wood 45
Gloy Viaduct 106, 107, 109
Great Glen 7, 8, 57, 72, 103, 104, 107, 108
Great Glen Water Park 110
Great Glen Water Park, 110
Great Glen Way 106, 110, 111, 113
Greenhill Junction 89

H

Hall Street, Campbeltown **119**, 121, **121, 122**
Heathers Bed and Breakfast Guest House 109
Highland Boundary Fault 7, 49, 81, 87
Hillhead aqueduct 73
'Hungry hoose' 123

I

Inchbuie 55
Invergarry 8, 106, 108, 110-112
Invergarry Station 109-111, **111**
Invergloy, bridge at **109**
Invergloy Halt 106, 109
Invergloy House 109
Inverness. 7, 8, 57, 103, 104, 108, 110, 115

J

Jamestown **93**
John Anderson 9, 14, 15, 17, 23, 28, 31, 37, 40, 51, 57, 58, 61, 69
John Napier, 83
John Thomas 81

K

Keil 66
Keltie Water 20
Kelty Water 84
Kelvin Valley West Junction 74
Kendrum Burn 28, 43
Kendrum Viaduct 28, 43
Kenmore 52, 56
Kentallen 60, 66
Kentallen Station 66, **67**
Kevin Costner 103
Kilchuimen 114
Kilkerran Road 122
Killearn 72, 73, 81, 82, **83**
Killearn New Station 82
Killearn Old 82
Killin 9, 15, 16, 18, 27, 32, 50-53, 55, 56
Killin Junction 18, 27, 32, 50, **50**, 52, 53, **54**, 55, 56
Killin Pugs 52
Killin Station 16, 32, 50, **55**
Kilmarnock 22, 41
Kilmaronock 95
Kilsyth 74
Kincaid Print Works 74
Kingshouse 16, 18, 26, 27
Kingshouse Halt 26

Kingshouse platform **27**
Kinlochleven 9, 58, 67
Kintyre 7, 9, 117, 118, 120
Kintyre Nurseries 123
Kippen 92, 99, 100
Kippen Station 100, **100**
Kippen Vine 100
Kirkintilloch 8, 9, 71-73
Kirkintilloch Station 73
Kirkton Glen 26

L
Ladyland's Platform 99
Ladyland's siding 99
Laggan 110
Laggan Farm 25
Laggan Locks 106, 110
Laggan Swing Bridge 110
Landslide on C&OR **30**
Lanfine Hospital. 74
Larbert 13
Ledaig 62, 63
Ledcharrie Burn 53
Ledcharrie Farm 26, 53
Ledcharrie Viaduct 33
Leitirfearn 112
Lennox Castle 77
Lennoxtown 72, 73, 75-77
Lennoxtown (Old) 72, 77
Lennoxtown Print Works 76, 77
Lennoxtown Station 76, **76**
Lenzie 71, 74, 80
Lenzie Junction 71-73
Letterfinlay 106
Letterfinlay Lodge Hotel 106, 110
Light Railway Act 117
Lilyburn Print Works 75
Limecraigs 118, 122
Lintmill 119, 121, 124
Lismore 62, 65
Lix Toll 27, 53, 54
Loch Achray 88
Lochan Larig Eala 31
Lochan Lairig Cheile 31

Loch Awe 17
Loch Creran 58, 59, 63
Loch Doine 26
Loch Earn 22, 27, 29, 30, 39-41, 43, 44, **45**, 47
Lochearnhead 9, 15, 16, 26-29, 32, 40-43
Lochearnhead Station 16, 29, 44, **44**
Lochearnhead Viaduct 29, 30, 43, 44, **45**
Loch Etive 14, 17, 58, 61
Loch Iubhair 35
Loch Katrine 72, 79, 87, 88
Loch Laich 65
Loch Leven 58, 59, 66-68
Loch Linnhe 57, 66
Loch Lochy 107-110
Loch Lomond 7, 8, 14, 22, 36, 71, 72, 79, 83, 89, 91, 95
Loch Long 22, 36
Loch Lubnaig 22, 24-26
Loch Ness 104, 114, 115
Loch Oich 106, 110, 112
Loch Oich side water drainage channel **112**
Loch Oich tunnel **112**
Loch Tay 9, 16, 22, 51-53, 55-57
Loch Tay Station 56
Loch Tay Station site **56**
Loch Treig 9
Loch Uanagan 113
Loch Voil 26
Lord Burton 103-105, 110, 115
Lovat Arms Hotel 105
Luggie Water 73, **74**
Luib 16-18, 26, 32-34
Luib Station 33, **34**, 35
Luib Station water tower base **34**
Luib Viaduct 32, 33, 53
Luib Viaduct abutments **33**

M

Machrihanish 117-119, 121, 124, 125
Machrihanish Airfield 120, 123
Machrihanish Bay 118
Machrihanish Farm 119
Machrihanish Farm Halt 121
Machrihanish Golf Course 118

Military pillbox, Gartmore Station **86**
Mallaig 7, 41
Marquis of Breadalbane 51
Menteith Hills 84, 87
'Mersey Mammoth' 64
Methven Junction 39
Mey's Siding 99
Millfaid 95
Milngavie 80, 90
Milton of Campsie 72-74, **75**
Milton of Campsie Station. 74
Milton of Campsie Station site **75**
Monty Python 20, 65, 80
Morven 66
Moss Road 119, 121
Mull of Kintyre 120

N

National Cycle Route No.7 27, 28, 73
Nevis 107
North Connel 60, 62
North Connel Station 62
North Laggan 106
North Ledaig 62
North Moy 123

O

Oban 7, 9, 13, 14, 17, 18, 21, 36, 39, 41, 42, 59, 62, 117
Ogle Burn 30, 44

P

Pass of Brander 17
Pass of Leny 15, 23
Perth, 7, 39
Pig Rock 48
Plantation 119, 121, 123
Port Appin 58, 65
Portnacroish 65
Port of Menteith 92, 99
Port of Menteith Station 99, **99, 100**
Pots of Gartness 83

137

Q

Queen Elizabeth Forest Park 88

R

River Balvag 25, 26
River Dochart 33, 35, 51, 53, 55
River Duror 66
River Earn 48, 49
River Endrick 82, 90, 95, 96
River Fillan 36, 37
River Garry 112
River Gloy 106
River Kelvin 73, 74
River Lednock 49
River Lochay 52, 56
River Oich 106, 114, 115
River Spean 106, 107, 115
River Teith 20, 23
Robert Cunninghame Graham 86
Rob Roy Way 18, 23, 27, 28
Rock Cottages. 25
Rowantreefauld Cottages 76

S

Sawdust Path 49
'Shaky Toun' 49
Shuna Castle 66
Shuna Island 66
Sir Walter Scott 8, 9, 88
Skye Bridge 112
Spean Bridge 104, 106, 107, 109
Spean Bridge Junction 106
Spean Bridge Station 106, 115
Spean Bridge Viaduct 106
Spean Gorge 109
St Fillans 29, 40-42, 44, 45, 48
St Fillans Hill 47
St Fillans Station 46, **47**
St Fillans tunnel **46**
Stirling 7-9, 13, 18, 19, 35, 36, 39, 71, 86, 90, 92, 99, 100

Stirling Castle 90
Stirling Council 30, 91
Stockbridge Farm 19
Strathblane 73, 76, 79, 80
Strathblane Hills 80
Strathblane Station 78, **78**
Strath Fillan 35, 37
Strathkelvin Walkway 73
Strathyre 15, 16, 18, 23, 25, 26, 45
Strathyre Heron **25**
Strathyre Station 25, 26
Stuc a' Chroin 28

T

'Tannochbrae' **22**
Tarbert 117
Tarbet 36
Taymouth Castle 51
the 'Laggan' 117, 118
'The 39 Steps' 52
'The Guns of Navarone' 107
'The Lady of the Lake' 88
Thomas Telford 108
Tomaig Bank 123
Tomaig Road 123, **123**
Tom Morris 118
Trodigal 119, 121
Trossachs 7-9, 13, 71, 72, 80, 81, 85, 87-89, 91
Tullybannocher Viaduct 49
Tyndrum 17, 36

U

Ugadale Arms Hotel 118, 124, **124**
Underwood Chemical Works 76
'Unique Bridge' **74**
Uplawmoor Station 22
Upper Strathearn Valley 39, 40

V

Vale of Leven 8, 89-92

W

Wallace Monument 101
Wemyss Bay 41
Wester Lix 54
West Machrihanish Farm 124
William Whitelaw 105
William Wordsworth 88

X

Y

Z

Alasdair Wham is the author of the very popular series on exploring the 'lost railway' network of Scotland. He is a Depute Head Teacher at a large Ayrshire Secondary School and is married with four sons.